D1399178

NATIONAL ASSOCIATION
OF INDEPENDENT SCHOOLS

SCHOOL LEADERSHIP
FOR THE FUTURE

Leading an Independent School

Thomas R. Hoerr

ISBN: 1-893021-77-7

Printed in the United States of America.

The National Association of Independent Schools represents approximately 1,400 independent private schools in the United States and other countries. All are accredited, non-discriminatory, nonprofit organizations governed by independent boards of trustees. NAIS's mission is to serve and strengthen member schools and associations by "articulating and promoting high standards of education quality and ethical behavior; to work to preserve their independence to serve the free society from which that independence derives; to advocate broad access for students by affirming the principles of diversity, choice, and opportunity."

For more information, go to the NAIS website at *www.nais.org*. To receive a listing of NAIS books, call (800) 793-6701 or (240) 646-7052.

Editors: Andrea Barbalich, Susan Hunt
Book Designer: Fletcher Design, Washington, DC

NATIONAL ASSOCIATION OF INDEPENDENT SCHOOLS

Mixed Sources
Product group from well-managed forests, controlled sources and recycled wood or fiber
www.fsc.org Cert no. SW-COC-002062
© 1996 Forest Stewardship Council

CONTENTS

FOREWORD

Each summer, NAIS offers a leadership training program for heads and their administrative teams called "Lessons in Leadership from the Battlefields of Gettysburg." I believe this institute is among our most successful for several reasons:

1. The institute's leader, Cole Kingseed, retired Army officer and history professor at West Point Academy, is a skilled and inspiring teacher.

2. The program's experiential approach, in which the participants walk the battlefield and troubleshoot decisions made by leaders under fire, is the best means for teaching adults, as it is for teaching students.

3. Heads bring members of their leadership team, which enables colleagues to learn together and also to reinforce the lessons once they return to campus.

4. The NAIS "case study" approach is included in the program, making the battlefield illustrations real in the school context.

The major players during the battle of Gettysburg all played key roles in the outcome of this turning point in the Civil War. Joshua Lawrence Chamberlain, professor of rhetoric and commander of the 1st Maine (and later governor of Maine and president of Bowdoin College) illustrates perfectly the nature of the high IQ/high EQ (emotional intelligence quotient) leader. A scene from the film *Gettysburg* (based on the novel *The Killer Angels* by Michael Shaara) illustrates the point: When 120 deserters arrive from another Maine regiment, Chamberlain's first remark to them is, "When did you last eat?" He gives them choices, but only to a point ("You are coming with us"), and firmly reminds them why they enlisted, what their common duty is now, and that they are fighting for one another. Chamberlain's education, intellect, and rhetorical skills framed his communication and won over the men's minds, but his visible caring for his soldiers, even the deserters, won over their hearts. How can school leaders develop the Chamberlain-like EQ skills that are key to successful leadership?

Communication is a frequent theme in the deconstruction of leadership lessons at Gettysburg. A classic miscommunication occurred when a Confederate commander, Richard Ewell, misinterpreted Robert E. Lee's instruction to take and hold Cemetery Ridge "if practicable" to mean that he should use his discretion. As it turned out, Lee's true intent was to communicate the order "Take the hill at any cost." Some would argue that it was Lee's communication failure that lost the battle and changed the course of the war. How often do school heads fail to make certain that their direct reports understand their intent?

Then there is the case of the Union commander, Daniel Sickles, a hot head and outsider (the only non-West Point officer in George Meade's command group) but also a man with many political friends and connections who continually pulled his feet out of the fire with his superiors. (Sickles was infamous for murdering his wife's lover and was exonerated by the first successful appeal to the "temporary insanity" plea.) At Gettysburg, Sickles saw an opportunity, ignored direct orders, improvised, and jeopardized the entire Union line. One school takeaway: Mavericks often bring fresh perspective and creative solutions. But what should you do if they become loose cannons or renegades? A second school takeaway: How do you balance the benefit a maverick brings to the table (as an antidote to groupthink) with the cost (since forgiving this person's misdeeds is demoralizing to others)?

At Gettysburg, we also learn from key moments: Lee's dressing down and then redirecting of General J.E.B. Stuart after he arrived late to the battle; Lee's "bet the farm" strategy on the battle's third day ("Pickett's Charge"); and the dilemma this forced on Lee's second-in-command: How hard do you challenge your boss when he's never been wrong before? How vigorously do you pursue your boss's strategy if you think it catastrophic? These, too, are lessons for school leaders to consider.

All of which brings us to Tom Hoerr's work, *School Leadership for the Future*, which answers the questions above and many more.

This remarkably well-structured and well-conceived book is basically a story, filled with concrete examples, about how to lead a school well. It answers all the questions that intimidate the neophyte and confound the veteran: How do you delegate and empower others? How do you energize, "manage up," and lead the board toward more strategic and productive work? How do you match your style with the school culture you inherit or, harder yet, guide the culture in new directions? How do you create a true leadership team whose collective knowledge and intelligence are greater than the sum of its individual parts? How do you use surveys, evaluations, and other tools to get useful feedback and redirect as needed? How should marketing work for the school? What's the head's role in development and finance?

Tom's book answers these questions very well, with guidance rooted in his own vast experience as a school leader and his research in the field. When I was a Boy Scout, I remember using the *Boy Scout Handbook* as my guide to everything I needed to know. Tom has written the equivalent guide for school leaders. Current heads will want to read this book as a reality check. Other school leaders and administrators will benefit from its insights. Prospective heads will want to read it before their first Search Committee interview.

NAIS is indebted to Tom for what is certain to become, along with our *Trustee Handbook*, a classic publication.

Patrick F. Bassett
President
National Association of Independent Schools
February 2009

INTRODUCTION

As I complete this book, I am serving in my 27th year as the head of an independent school. Prior to performing this role, I served as a public school principal and teacher. Throughout my career, my penchant for writing has helped me try to make sense of issues. For the past five years, I have been fortunate to write a bimonthly column for *Educational Leadership* called "The Principal Connection." For better and worse, this keeps me probing and analyzing. The "better" is obvious: Writing causes me to reflect and think about what we — what I — should do. The "worse" may be less obvious, but it's just as powerful: Writing causes me to reflect and think about what we — what I — am not doing or what I am doing that isn't helpful.

The "better and worse" applies to this book, too. It has been both helpful and humbling — helpful because it has caused me to read and think about important issues and has enabled me to interview scores of other school heads, humbling because it has forced me to come face to face with my own shortcomings. Believe me, it is far easier to write about what should be done than it is to do it! I believe I am a better head of school because of my thinking and writing, but I am definitely aware of the disparity between my preaching and my practicing.

The audience for this book includes other heads of school, and I have addressed aspects of leadership that are unique to independent schools. Working with a school board sets the tone appropriately, but I have also covered the areas of marketing, admissions, and development. The book's scope is broader, however, and is also addressed to principals of charter, public, and religious schools, as well as those who hope to run a school and those who study leadership. Much of what I've written is applicable to schools and school leaders everywhere. Issues of school culture, faculty development and collegiality, and human diversity exist in every school.

My purpose in writing this book is not to duplicate other resources. In looking at governance, for example, BoardSource offers wonderful materials and rich thoughts, as does the National Association of Independent Schools (NAIS). My intent is to approach these topics from the perspective of one who runs a school. My thinking is necessarily framed by my own experiences.

As Daniel Goleman notes in his book, *Social Intelligence*, "Studies comparing superb leaders with mediocre ones have found that the competencies that distinguish the best from the worst in human services have little or nothing to do with medical knowledge or technical skill, and everything to do with social and emotional intelligence."* I have learned this as well: Regardless of the type of school, it is leadership that makes the difference. Strong leaders help everyone do a better job, whatever that job may be. My hope is that this book will serve as a tool for improvement. It has been that for me. My journey has not always been an easy one, and it has never been boring. I have led schools long enough that I have a list of mistakes on which I can reflect and from which I can learn.

My coffee mug reads "Often wrong, never in doubt" for good reason. While I am responsible for any errors and all shortcomings in this book, the insights and connections are due to many others who have worked with me and patiently given their support. To begin, thanks go to everyone in the New City School community. I am indebted to our students and their parents, our board of trustees and friends, and our remarkable faculty. Each day I come to school knowing that I will learn something new. This really is a special place.

---

* For this and all other published works referred to in this book, please see the Bibliography.

Appreciation goes to Nancy Raley and Pat Bassett of NAIS for their confidence and encouragement. Special appreciation goes to my editor, Andrea Barbalich, for making all my words read more coherently and smoothly (no easy task!), and to Susan Hunt for giving the manuscript a second review (still no easy task!). Thanks to Karleen, B.J., and Casper, my wife and pooches, for their support. Thanks for their faith in me to Mrs. Mayfield, my first-grade teacher, to Pauline Wolff, the first secretary who worked with me, and to Rita Curtis, my mom. And thanks to all the major distractions in my life, including my book club and all the weekend b-ball hoopsters. Thank you, everyone!

Tom Hoerr
February 2009

■

CHAPTER 1

THE HEAD OF SCHOOL

WHY HEAD A SCHOOL?

It's not as though leading a school is the perfect job. Sure, each day presents a new challenge, but fighter pilots and talk-show hosts seem to have pretty interesting jobs, too. It's possible that being a professional athlete is more fun than leading a school. From a distance, the thought of getting paid to play seems like a real treat. And certainly there are some jobs that are more rewarding than being a head of school. A friend of mine is a transplant surgeon, and I can't begin to imagine the emotions that surround him after a successful operation. But it's the combination of factors that distinguish the job of head of school. I'm not sure how many other jobs are as interesting, fun, and rewarding.

Leading a school is never boring. (Indeed, there are times when I think a bit of boredom would be welcome.) That's because the job is always changing. Each year brings new students and teachers and a different curricular emphasis; in each new year, we must address changing perceptions in the community and on the board. This means that the head of school has the opportunity to be — indeed, I think the obligation to be — a perpetual learner. Roland Barth, the author of *Improving Schools from Within*, once suggested that the sign above the principal's office should say "Head Learner." Those of us who lead schools need to be continual learners, and it should be obvious to those around us that we are.

Leading a school can be fun, too. Children's smiles are infectious. The joy and wonder of six-year-olds losing baby teeth or 16-year-olds going to the prom never get old; it's always inspiring to watch students learn and grow. Sometimes you can witness the moment of inspiration take place when students are making a presentation in class. You see them gather themselves, gaining confidence and aplomb as they make eye contact with their audience. Or it might happen while a student is playing on the soccer field or performing in the band. Perhaps it takes place after a student has struggled to decipher an algebraic formula or write a five-paragraph essay. Each spring, I play our school's grade-level champions in a chess tournament, and watching the kids think and compete is always a treat, even when I lose (actually, especially when I lose). The settings for student growth are as varied as our schools and the students themselves. What remains the same, regardless of setting, is that working with students is tremendous fun. It keeps us young (on most days).

And while it's not the same as performing transplant surgery, working with children is also incredibly rewarding. Most school heads can recount the times when graduates returned to our campuses to share their successes and thank us for the role we played in their development. But our rewards are not limited to seeing our students grow. Teachers and students' parents often make a point of telling me that they appreciate the role I've played in their development. In good schools, everyone learns and grows.

That's not to say that running a school is without headaches and frustrations (and sometimes the headaches and frustrations receive paychecks that I've signed!). There are days when our job is neither interesting nor rewarding and times when it isn't much fun either. When that happens, I remind myself that it takes the bad days to appreciate the good ones. In fact, the complexity and challenges of the job are what make it so rewarding.

I once asked a school administrator to cite the hardest part of his job. Without hesitation he replied, "There's no one part that's particularly hard, but what's really difficult is balancing everything." Balance is the key to our jobs: balancing the competing and sometimes conflicting interests of students, parents, and staff members; balancing curricular thrusts; balancing the budget; and certainly balancing our job and our lives. Not only is the balance elusive in each of these areas, but once found, it can easily disappear. Achieving balance is always a temporary victory; the tensions of focus and time remain inherent in the job.

THE ROLE OF LEADERSHIP

In *Social Intelligence*, Daniel Goleman says, "Leaders need to realize that they themselves set much of the emotional tone that flows through the halls of their organizations, and that this in turn has a consequence for how well the collective objectives are met — whether the outcome is measured in achievement test scores, sales goals, or retention of nurses." There's no doubt that leaders make the difference in organizations, perhaps particularly in schools, where the goals can be so complex and subjective. Effective leaders possess strong skills and vision, but these qualities alone do not set them apart. Rather, truly good leaders make the difference by developing the people with whom they work.

It is this appreciation for employee growth — the willingness to take the time and spend the energy to develop those around them — that sets the tone to which Goleman refers. Whether the organization is nonprofit or for-profit, the consensus is that leaders must focus on both the ends and the means, the *what* and the *how*. Leaders have an obligation to establish priorities and create structures and processes that will nurture their employees' professional growth. Leaders invest in their employees.

Please don't misunderstand me: Schools should be designed for students. But focusing on teacher growth supports that priority. Creating a setting in which teachers continue to grow will result in increased student learning. I know that sometimes it can be hard to remember this. For example, professional development funds are often the first to be restricted when a budget is tight. But the fact remains that when developing employees becomes the goal, everyone gains. It's not enough to focus only on raising scores on test X or helping graduates get accepted into school Y or Z. Those are appropriate and laudable goals, but they cannot be the only goals. School leaders must also focus on helping all their employees learn. Regardless of how good our faculty members are this September, they need to be better the following year. It is true for leaders as well: Regardless of how well we perform at our jobs today, we must perform better next year. When we improve, our schools improve, and when that happens our students' successes in test scores, in school acceptances, and in life will follow.

Peter Drucker talked about the necessary investment in employees years ago when he coined the term "knowledge worker." Drucker was observing that the balance of power in the workplace was shifting. No longer were employees beholden to businesses and manufacturers who owned the technology and production systems on which their jobs depended. Instead, employees carried the necessary knowledge and skills in their heads. This caused employees to receive greater respect and a different kind of relationship to evolve. Top-down, hierarchical bosses who relied on one-way communication became anachronisms. While bosses were and are still in charge, today they understand that helping employees grow is an important part of their responsibility.

This same thrust of leaders empowering their employees is reflected in much of today's writing on leadership. The philosophy is shared by Roland Barth, Jim Collins, Steven Covey, Sally Helgesen, Frances Hesselbein, Patrick Lencioni, and Peter Senge, among others. It is also shown when leadership is approached a bit differently, by looking at it through the prism of the workplace, as in Richard Florida's book, *The Rise of the Creative Class … and How It's Transforming Work, Leisure, Community and Everyday Life*. Florida refers to the "no-collar workplace" and says that workers "work more independently and find it much harder to cope with incompetent managers and bullying bosses. We trade job security for autonomy."

THE IMPORTANCE OF THE HEAD OF SCHOOL

"Why do you want to be the head of an independent school?" That question was first put to me years ago. One of two finalists for the job, I was asked this at a parent forum. I had been a teacher and was a public school principal at the time, and my answer came easily.

"Simple," I said. "I want to make a difference." While educators in every role and at every level make a difference for students, I already knew that leading a school gave me more opportunities to make a difference than my teaching did. I also suspected that heading an independent school would give me far greater autonomy than I had experienced as a public school principal. In my response, I talked about the role of the head of school in helping everyone grow.

My answer must have been satisfactory because a week later, I was notified that the position was mine. While that was the first time I was asked the question, it wasn't the last. I am often asked why it is that I head an independent school instead of being a superintendent, central office administrator, public school principal, or higher education faculty member. To my mind, the answer is still easy. This role offers the best of all worlds. My job is large enough that I can influence hundreds of students and scores of teachers each year but small enough to allow me to be part of a community of learners.

Unlike when I was a public school principal, being a head of school means that I have my hand in everything. School heads are responsible for curriculum, instruction, and professional development to be sure, but that's just the beginning. We are also routinely involved in issues of finance, buildings and grounds, diversity, athletics, health and safety, financial aid, marketing, development, supervision, community outreach, legal matters, and human resources.

This means that we work on topics that are new to us. Personally, this has caused me to become much more knowledgeable about a variety of issues. It both amazes and delights me, for example, that I have become well-versed enough that I can actually enjoy attending Finance Committee meetings. Likewise, in recent years we've been spending a good deal of energy on marketing; this, too, is an area that I find quite engaging. As a public school principal, I would not have had the opportunity to learn about or participate in these areas.

In addition, the governance structure of independent schools means that school heads work closely with a board of trustees composed of many adults who are not educators. Working with and learning from non-educators who have expertise in finance, law, architecture, marketing, development, health care, diversity, or management is always interesting. Sometimes, I'm very aware of how a person's training and background influence perception of issues. At other times, I am struck by how similarly people with varying backgrounds approach certain problems (and at other times, I am surprised at how differently issues can be perceived!).

Growth opportunities aside, being responsible for everything — okay, maybe not everything, but it sure feels like that some days — has its drawbacks, too. Realistically, this range of responsibilities means that there is no way that any head of school can have all the knowledge and information necessary to do the job really well. (Search committees, heads, and boards of trustees need to know this.) Although some frustration accompanies this reality, the wide span of responsibilities forces us to delegate. I have talked with many successful school heads, and although their backgrounds, styles, and schools vary, they all have the ability to delegate often and well.

Delegation, as I know firsthand, is another area that is much easier to write about than to do well. Assigning tasks and responsibilities to others is one thing, but actually letting go of these tasks and responsibilities is another. Letting go implies an openness about solutions and a willingness to allow employees to come up with a product or strategy that might be different from the one you would have created. As difficult as letting go can be, however, it's necessary — not only because we can't master all areas and don't have the time to do everything but because it's important for staff members' growth. Daniel Goleman remarks on this phenomenon: "One way to promote positive expectations is to let others take the lead in setting their own goals, rather than dictating the terms and manner of their development. This communicates the belief that the employees have the capacity to be the pilot of their own destiny."

Finally, although it may seem obvious, it needs to be noted that being responsible for the entire enterprise carries with it a level of stress. Precisely because we are involved in all aspects of a school, we can share in successes throughout the building and across the campus. The dark side of this is that sometimes it can be very hard to let go of all the responsibilities. Even after so many years as a head of school, it's difficult for me not to feel that everything is my responsibility. (Of course, that's because it is!) Because I am responsible for all personnel, because I ultimately sign off on every educational issue, and because I work with the board on matters of policy, it all rests at my feet. Sometimes it can be hard to share in the triumphs when I am intimately aware of the shortcomings. After all, when the sunlight is brightest, the shadows are darkest. Depending on their personalities and schools, heads may need to work against the tendency to always focus on what isn't done as well, as quickly, or as inexpensively as they would like.

A LEARNING COMMUNITY

Peter Senge says that a learning organization is one "that is continually expand-ing its capacity to create its future." There may have been a day — perhaps in the halcyon 1980s? — when this was not the case and when school leaders did not have to be so focused on the future. While we didn't know it at the time, life was relatively easy. We opened our doors and, by and large, students came to us. Educational accountability was less of an issue then, so we enrolled children, often descendants of the privileged, and did our thing, whatever that was, and students prospered. Those seem like distant times.

Today just about everything has changed — and continues to change. The challenges facing us are more complex than any of us can address alone. The increased scrutiny of education and educators (exacerbated by the No Child Left Behind Act, which influences us whether or not we are bound to it), coupled with the contagious skepticism of Generation X parents, has changed the home-school relationship. Whether they are the "helicopter parents" who hover, the "Volvo mafia" who gather in the school's parking lot, or the parents of a five-year-old who want to be sure their daughter will attend Harvard, parents are no longer inhibited about asking, pushing, and pushing again. Often parents feel this is their responsibility. They've learned that they must be outspoken advocates of their and their family's interests everywhere else in society, from monitoring their physicians to overseeing the cable television installers, so why should it be any different when they interact with schools?

But the evolution in parent-school relations is only the beginning. Both education and society are changing at such a rate that merely being responsive is not adequate. School leaders must look around the corner and anticipate the

LOOKING AROUND THE CORNER: QUESTIONS FOR THE NEXT 20 YEARS

- How will technology change how we learn?
- How will increased global economic competitiveness change us?
- How will our country's increasing diversity affect us?
- How will environmental ("green") considerations change what we do?
- How can we strike the balance between lower-order and higher-order thinking skills?
- How can we foster creativity in our students and faculty?

Independent school leaders must anticipate these same questions and more:

- How will student demographics affect us?
- How can we market ourselves?
- How will increasing tuition costs influence us?
- How will the proliferation of choices in the public school sector affect us?
- How should our mission evolve?

forces that will have an impact on education and on their roles in the future. Some of the questions that will frame education over the next 20 years are listed in the sidebar on the previous page.

The best answers to these questions are beyond the capacity of any one of us. In fact, questions like these are never answered definitively; once an answer is obtained, it begins to be history, and the question must be addressed anew. Wise school leaders will continue to ask these questions in order to forge communication, gain understanding, and develop specific strategies.

Chapter 5 is devoted to faculty collegiality, but I would be remiss if I did not note the importance of collegiality here as well. The main tenet of faculty collegiality is that the adults must grow and learn if children are to grow and learn; learning must pervade the organization. It is hard to find anyone who disagrees with the notion of collegiality, but it is difficult to find schools in which it is practiced well. Teachers are used to closing their doors and teaching, and administrators are used to respecting the fact that good teaching takes place behind closed doors. Unfortunately, everyone loses when this is the unwritten expectation.

LEGITIMACY

Rita Bornstein's 2003 work, *Legitimacy in the Academic Presidency*, is quite relevant to heads of schools. Her focus is on higher education, but the issues that are addressed and the relationships among the protagonists — leaders of institutions, faculty members, members of the board of trustees, and members of the community — are virtually the same as those found in independent schools. As a result, the parallels are remarkable. It is worthwhile to examine Bornstein's conclusions and see how they translate to elementary and secondary school settings.

Bornstein analyzed the college presidency to determine how legitimacy is gained, how legitimacy is used, and how presidential succession evolves. She argues that today's leaders must rely more on persuasion and trust and less on mandates. The power of the leaders she describes is derived from their personal and professional legitimacy, not from their hierarchical position. Bornstein's comments describing college presidents are also appropriate for heads of schools. Several ideas from her book are worth focusing on:

- **"At the same time that constituents have expanded their expectations for a president, they have also reduced their tolerance for error."**

  Indeed, which school head has not felt that the stakes are higher and the margins for error are narrower than they used to be? From Watergate through Iraq, confidence in public officials has eroded. As a result, they — we — receive less trust, confidence, and benefit of the doubt. While this skepticism is especially characteristic of Generation X parents, it pervades society.

- **"Presidential legitimacy depends, in part, on the ability to manage an institution through environmental vicissitudes."**

  Leadership can be far less obvious when things are going well. Legitimacy is earned in tough times. A difficulty that long-standing, effective leaders may have is that they do their job so well and so easily that it appears effortless to outsiders. Because they are able to anticipate and plan, many problems never rise to the surface. It can be hard to appreciate a leader's skills when they're not obvious because they are used with such subtlety.

- **"Presidents who do not have their hands on the day-to-day academic issues in their institutions ... lose academic credibility with both external and internal constituents."**

  As do college presidents, school heads vary in their degree of involvement with curriculum and instruction. However, even when this area is delegated to others, everyone must understand that it remains the highest priority for the head of school. Heads must find ways to ensure that there can be no doubt about this.

- "[T]o gain legitimacy, a president must demonstrate a leadership style that comports with the culture of the institution."

  Perhaps the distinguishing characteristic between public and private schools is that independent schools, by design, all have a unique mission and culture. In large part, leadership is the ability to manage and change a school's culture. (School culture is the focus of Chapter 3.)

Bornstein also notes that "cultural fit and management expertise are identified as the core elements of legitimacy." When a candidate is applying for a job, the degree of cultural fit should be obvious to both the candidate and the search committee, and over time this becomes a moot issue. Thus, management expertise is the key. For heads of school, this has two components: expertise in education and expertise in management. As noted, expertise in education is something that cannot be fully delegated, nor should it be. Heads of school should have a passion about how children learn and how schools should be organized to enhance that learning.

Expertise in management includes the ability to delegate, certainly, along with the ability to know what you don't know and the candor to admit it. Good leaders know what they don't know and then find ways to tap into a skill set that will help them accomplish the task. It may be involving faculty members in new and different roles; it may be pulling volunteers into the problem-solving and decision-making process; it may be hiring individuals with talents that complement those of the administrative team. The important issue is whether the task was accomplished, not necessarily who accomplished it. Good leaders always work to pinpoint what it is they don't know and then figure out how to respond. I often think that a good gauge of someone's intellect and leadership is how many questions he or she asks.

HEADS VS. PRINCIPALS

The autonomy I referred to in talking about why I wanted to lead an independent school in that job interview years ago carries many benefits. The obvious benefit

— a school's capacity to set its own mission — is one of the hallmarks of an independent school. This means that I work with my faculty to find new and better ways to help students learn and grow. We aren't bound by the actions and decisions of another school up the street or down the road. It allows us to fashion a course that we believe is right. That's a wonderful motivator!

As an independent school head, I also have the opportunity to work with a board of trustees. I have worked with many boards over the years, and each is unlike any other, but all share a desire to help the school improve. The board members' backgrounds and perspectives are all quite different, and I find myself learning from them, both individually and collectively. I made the case in my book, *The Art of School Leadership*, that all schools, public and private, should have advisory boards. Whether these are formally convened groups (as is the case at my school) or simply a collection of outsiders with whom a school leader calls and consults regularly is not important. What matters is that principals and school heads tap into the perceptions and skills of others. Independent schools are at an advantage in doing this because they each have a board of trustees, but that is not enough. School heads need to be constantly identifying others who can be helpful to their school and to them personally. Regardless of our experience or knowledge, we all need to learn from others.

In no way do I mean to be critical of public or charter school principals. I remember all too well the additional challenges I faced when I ran a public school. From having zero control over who attended my school to having limited input into our curriculum to being given minimal opportunities to select faculty, I often felt that I was given responsibility without authority. To be certain, public school principals must surmount some additional hurdles. And independent school heads have their own endemic hurdles, such as managing enrollment and raising funds. Rather than looking at how the roles are different, I think it's best to focus on the many variables and challenges they have in common.

SUMMARY

We are all prisoners of our history and biases. Mine inform both my practice and how I think and write about it. Here a few of my unshakable viewpoints.

- **Leadership is about relationships.** Simply put, people work with us and for us because they believe in us and care about us. Taking the time to build and maintain relationships is a must.

- **Everyone grows in a good organization, and the job of the leader is to make that growth possible.** Our jobs should enable us to achieve this, and we need to start with ourselves. Heads of school need to visibly model growth.

- **We all learn best in a constructivist manner.** Early childhood teachers know that young children learn experientially, through engagement and by creating meaning. It's no different for adults. We learn better when we interact with others and are part of a learning process.

- **Mistakes are necessary.** Making the same old mistake isn't smart; we all know that. But not making any mistakes isn't smart either. A lack of mistakes means a lack of risk-taking and an absence of learning. Smart people learn from their mistakes. Making *new* mistakes is the key: That implies that learning and progress are taking place. A philosophy of MNM (Make New Mistakes) throughout an organization means that employees are comfortable trying new strategies.

- **Heads work with, not for, boards.** Of course, heads do officially work for boards. In fact, a head of school is the only employee of a board. That said, in good schools the relationship between the head of school and the board of trustees is characterized by mutual respect and collaboration.

Before reading any further, I suggest that you step back a bit and think about your biases. What biases do you have about how leaders lead, adults and students learn, and organizations function? With which of mine do you agree or disagree?

CHAPTER 2

■

GOVERNANCE
Working with a Board

ENGAGEMENT IS THE GOAL

I recently resigned from the board of directors of a local nonprofit children's agency. This organization serves children in wonderful ways and makes a positive difference in their lives. My stated reason for resigning was that my life was too full and I needed to prioritize and cut back on my commitments. That's true, but it's only a part of the picture.

You see, even after serving on the board for a couple of years, I wasn't engaged. I didn't feel needed or valued in a unique way. Oh, I attended board meetings and committee meetings. I listened and offered my thoughts, and I wrote checks to the organization. But the organization never snagged me. If it had, my priorities would have been different, and I would have cut back on some other activity.

There is a lesson here for heads of independent schools: Never make the mistake of assuming that trustees will give their all simply because the cause

— the school — is so important. After all, there are many worthy causes in the world, and a trustee could wisely choose to devote time and resources to any of them. That is why keeping board members invested in the school is an important part of every head's job. This responsibility doesn't fall to the head alone. Certainly it is a major responsibility of the board president, and chairs of various board committees do this, too. Still, the head of school must work to keep board members interested and involved.

The head's relationship with the board of trustees is a complicated one, to be sure, even in the best of times. As the title of this chapter indicates, I am fond of saying that the head works *with* the board, rather than *for* the board. Of course, as I've said, the head does work for the board. But by changing prepositions, I hope to convey that the relationship between the head and the board of trustees should be one of mutual support. This kind of relationship does not come easily or automatically; achieving it requires focus and effort. Heads of school are quick to talk, understandably, about how the board needs to support them, and it does. However, the head also needs to support the board.

SUPPORTING THE BOARD

This important responsibility begins with working to ensure that the school embodies and achieves its mission. Our resources — time, energy, and dollars — are always limited (and never sufficient), so every decision and priority must be examined through the lens of the school's mission. The board of trustees approves the mission, and the head must lead the school community in embracing it.

Supporting the board also means going along with board decisions and publicly supporting them, providing administrative support for board committees, and engaging board members. In collaboration with the chair of the board, the head's job is to keep board members excited about the school's mission and working actively for the school's improvement. NAIS President Patrick Bassett talks about the board's three R's: raising students, raising image, and raising money. An important aspect of the head's role is to help make it possible for board members to meet these obligations.

In *Social Behavior: Its Elementary Forms*, George Homans noted that social behavior is an exchange. Simply put, we remain only in relationships that are beneficial to us, those in which we receive more positives than negatives. Fortunately, relationships are not zero-sum, so everyone in the relationship can realize gains simultaneously. While Homans focused on personal relationships, his point is even truer in volunteer relationships. After all, the incentives for staying in relationships are typically more powerful in personal and professional arenas than they are in volunteer settings. If we want board members to give us their enthusiasm, energy, and dollars, we need to help ensure that their participation on our board is both worthwhile to them and beneficial to us. Board members must have opportunities to make meaningful contributions and know that their presence makes a positive difference.

While this kind of engagement is a focus of the board chair and other board members as well, the head's role cannot be ignored. Connecting with board members should always be a goal of the head of school. The starting point, both obvious and elusive, for engaging board members is to know them and to understand their context, interests, and skills. Engagement comes when we work, when we care, and when we feel responsible.

Timothy Backous, head of Saint John's Preparatory School in Minnesota, has a theory: "Sixty percent of the week should be devoted to board members. I know it sounds excessive, but according to studies, the increased amount of time renders increased productivity and commitment." That percentage does seem high to me, but the point is well taken. Conventional wisdom among heads of school is that it's beneficial to have a one-on-one meeting with each board member every year. Realistically, however, this is often very difficult to accomplish. Heads have myriad other relationships that demand their attention. They are busy focusing on their teachers, support staff, students, students' parents, and administrators. Tending to board members may seem like the last thing they have time for. But when you consider the board's role in the success of the institution and the head of school, how can the head not invest the time that is needed to do this well?

To be sure, the roles that heads and chairs play can make communication even more difficult. "By virtue of their position, both individuals approach any conversation with a set of preconceptions that can cause them to not hear what the other is saying but to feed the other person's thoughts through their own personal meat grinder," says Billy Handmaker, head of Crossroads College Preparatory School in Missouri. "What comes out is something completely different from what the other meant." Both the head and the board chair need to be aware of this potential for misunderstanding, and both need to be good listeners.

If it is not realistic to have individual meetings with each board member, heads must still make a point of connecting with each one. They might accomplish this by working closely with board members on committees or by scheduling phone calls. "Scheduling" means that the time is determined in advance and that both the head and board member have set aside time to talk at length. (Where has technology taken us? I often find myself using e-mail to determine a time when I can have a phone conference with someone.) Regardless of how it's done, heads must get to know their board members. This knowledge allows heads to understand board members' expertise and appreciate their interests in order to help them become involved in productive ways — and keep them from getting involved in ways that are not helpful.

A quick way to judge whether or not board members are engaged is to consider the degree to which all board members are involved in the discussions during a board or committee meeting. If one or two people dominate the dialogue, if there's little conversation, or if the meeting primarily consists of reports being read, those are signs that most board members are not engaged. Board chairs and school heads share the responsibility for ensuring that meetings are interactive and interesting.

INTERESTS VS. RESPONSIBILITIES

I have noted that heads of school need to help ensure that board members' participation on the board is beneficial. The word "help" reflects that the head of school cannot — indeed, should not — do this alone. After all, the board chair is the board's leader, and one of the chair's important tasks is to work with board members and guide them productively and collaboratively. Yet sometimes, heads draw the lines of interest too narrowly and rigidly. They assume that their job is only to run the school and the chair's job is only to run the board. That's true, but it's also naive. The head of school and board chair are a team, and their interests both coincide and overlap.

It's essential that the chair and the head meet regularly. "I speak with the board chair every day," says Joan Lutton, head of the Cushman School in Florida. "That way, there are no surprises in either direction. I have been a head for almost 30 years and have always used this method. I think good communication is the key to good relationships in all arenas."

In my own case, I have worked with 10 board chairs. I have not been in daily communication with them unless a particular situation warranted it, but I made sure the communication was planned and frequent. Typically, this took place every couple of weeks over lunch or a late-morning cup of coffee. In addition, there have been conversations in the hall, discussions before and after other meetings, numerous phone calls, and many e-mails. School challenges and individual personalities differ over time, but the interplay between the chair's and head's roles is obvious. Regularly scheduled meetings allow each to draw from the other's ideas and strengths.

In these one-on-one meetings, I talk candidly with the board chair. I share our successes but also my fears, frustrations, worries, and problems. Mary Worch, head of Woods Academy in Maryland, agrees that it's vital to share both the bad and the good. "It is important that the head of school keep the board chair aware of percolating issues that may arise," she says. "No one likes to be blindsided."

Just as I am candid with the chair, the chair is candid with me and likewise doesn't hold back on fears, frustrations, worries, and problems. We listen and offer suggestions. While it's clear that we each have a primary area of responsibility, it's also clear that we each need to be knowledgeable about all aspects of the school. Sometimes, the chair will raise a concern about a board member who isn't involved enough (or may be too involved), and we'll brainstorm how to address the problem. Occasionally, we'll talk about an issue of joint responsibility — perhaps marketing efforts, a development strategy, or the school's participation in a community venture. At other times, I'll share a personnel or curriculum concern and ask for thoughts or inquire whether the chair feels it's appropriate to take the problem to the Executive Committee members for their input. These lines of interest overlap, but the lines of responsibility do not. I am not in charge of the board, and the board chair is not in charge of the school. We have our own leadership roles and responsibilities, but each of us gains from sharing and working with the other.

DISTRIBUTED INTELLIGENCE

The notion of "distributed intelligence" means that our intelligence is not limited to what is inside our skin. Rather, people with a strong distributed intelligence know how to identify and draw from the resources around them in solving problems. The term originated in describing how people use tools and technology to be "smarter," and it also holds in describing how smart people capitalize on the interpersonal talents and strengths of others. (One example of successfully using others as resources is Abraham Lincoln as captured in Doris Kearns Goodwin's book, *Team of Rivals*.) A good head will use her distributed intelligence to draw from the strengths of those with whom she works. While this primarily speaks to the head's relationships with other administrators and teachers, it also includes board members, led by the board chair.

Regardless of the chair's background — and having worked with 10 chairs, this has varied quite a bit for me — every chair has brought a strong commitment and unique perspective. None of the chairs I've served with has been a K–12 educator, so that alone has caused each of them to see things differently than

I do. In addition, all the chairs were parents of students who were attending or who had attended my school, so they also viewed issues from a parent's perspective. Finally, all had the responsibility for leading the board, and that framed their thinking. Sometimes, this difference in background and role engendered a disagreement, and that's okay. Indeed, as Gandhi said, "Honest disagreement is often a good sign of progress." In working with a board chair, the goal is not to see things the same way; it's to share openly and learn from each other.

MEETING MATTERS

Board meetings are those official times when boards govern; they receive information and take a formal position. If a board is functioning well, the bulk of its activities will take place at the committee level, and reports from committees regarding their progress and challenges are important parts of board meetings. That said, every committee should not report at every meeting. The board meetings should be characterized by good interaction, not just good listening (although good listening is important). The committees that need to report should be listed on the agenda so their reports can be planned: What does the board need to know? What actions does the board need to take? It can be effective to set a cap on the length of both the meeting and the individual committee reports. Whereas sometimes a time limit cannot be predicted, such as when the Finance Committee's report includes a recommendation for the following year's tuition, often committee chairs can give their report within five minutes. Providing background material in the board packet ahead of time can be helpful.

Another significant part of each board meeting is the head's oral report. This is the time for the head to share what is happening and to draw the board into thinking about today's victories and tomorrow's challenges. Board members should be knowledgeable about a school's programs, but the head cannot assume that they are and therefore should devote part of the report to talking about various programs and strategies. This kind of knowledge not only enhances board members' decision-making skills, but it gives them information that will enable them to respond effectively to a question or concern from a student's parent or a community member. Even if board members already see what's happening and understand the changes that are taking place, the head can use the report to pull back the curtain and share the rationale and infrastructure.

For example, my school has been implementing the theory of multiple intelligences for nearly 20 years. Even after all this time, the term "multiple intelligences," as well as our implementation strategies, can be confusing to our students' parents. If a board member is asked, "What does the term 'multiple intelligences' mean?" and cannot answer it comfortably, I will have a problem. Not only will the parent go away with more questions and less confidence, but my board member will feel uncertain and unhelpful. Part of my role, then, is giving enough information to enable board members to be successful when they are asked about the school. (Another part of my role — and the board chair's role, too — is to educate board members about those times when they should not answer a question or concern posed by a parent but should instead refer the parent to a teacher or to me. We should not assume that board members will know how to respond to a friend's question or the complaint of a colleague unless this has been discussed.)

The head's report is an opportunity to inform and establish credibility with the board. Everything is not always rosy even in the best-run school, so even though it may run counter to heads' tendencies to put everything in the best possible light, they should also include their worries and fears during their report. Doing so not only enables the board to help the head in solving the problems but also increases the head's credibility. The willingness to share a problem, and to sometimes invite the board into assisting with its solution, reflects well on the head of school. When no problems or challenges are raised, board members will naturally wonder whether the head is aware of what's happening and may decide to identify problems on their own.

In the past, for example, I've talked candidly with the board about a curriculum innovation that wasn't successful (schoolwide themes), about the slow progress of a capital campaign (raising money was more difficult than expected), and about the difficulty of balancing skill-based instruction with the quest for joyful learning. Similarly, there have been times when the board has gone into executive session to allow me to share a difficult personnel situation. In an executive session, non-board members are asked to leave the room and the board's minutes reflect only this transition: "The board went into executive session to discuss a personnel matter." At these times, I've shared the rationale behind a personnel decision, including my doubts and hesitations. I am always careful to remind the board that personnel decisions are my responsibility and that I am seeking input or informing them of a decision I have made. The board chair supports this and reminds everyone that the issue is confidential.

The head's report should help engage the board members. Board meetings should be interesting and, at times, fun. But board meetings should be far more than that. It is important for the board members to go beyond simply listening and responding. True engagement comes from interaction, participation, and achievement. Again, while the chair leads the board, the head should be instrumental in framing board meetings. (Additional thoughts about how to effectively lead meetings can be found in Chapter 8, "Making Faculty and Committee Meetings Meaningful," in *The Art of School Leadership*.)

GOVERNANCE EVOLVED

Richard Chait has taken the lead in thinking about how nonprofit boards should operate. A Harvard professor and frequent NAIS presenter, he is the coauthor, along with William Ryan and Barbara Taylor, of *Governance as Leadership: Reframing the Work of Nonprofit Boards*. (When referring to "Chait's work and thinking," I mean to include the work and thinking of all three coauthors.) Chait's position is that nonprofit boards operate in three modes of governance.

Type 1: The fiduciary mode, in which "boards are concerned primarily with the stewardship of tangible assets";

Type 2: The strategic mode, in which "boards create a strategic partnership with management"; and

Type 3: The generative mode, in which "boards provide a less recognized but critical source of leadership for the organization."

There is a hierarchy — boards progress to Type 3 governance — but as Chait notes, "When trustees work well in all three of these modes, the board achieves governance as leadership." Too often, however, boards remain at the Type 1 or 2 level: Boards review audits and hear how resources are allocated; boards look ahead and plan. While those functions are essential and need to happen routinely, Chait maintains that they are not adequate.

The Type 3 (generative) mode is characterized by going beyond questions of strategy. Sometimes this means framing the discussion by asking *why* questions and not settling for the *what* or even *how* questions. At board meetings, participants should interact, discussing issues and problems at a global-enough level so that patterns and values are articulated and examined. That kind of dialogue shouldn't be all that happens, of course, but it should be an integral part of the board's deliberations. These kinds of deliberations offer opportunities to engage all board members in meaningful discussion.

One way to start to move the board to this level of analysis is to begin meetings by discussing articles that were included in the board packet or mailed/e-mailed to members prior to the meeting. At two recent meetings, for example, my board spent 20 minutes discussing a series of articles on intelligence ("Intelligence in the Classroom," "What's Wrong with Vocational School?," and "Aztecs vs. Greeks") by Charles Murray that appeared in the *Wall Street Journal* on January 16, 17, and 18, 2007, respectively. We have also read and talked about articles on school governance and on child development. In each case, I led the discussion by asking questions and encouraging board members to first reflect on the questions and write personal notes and then discuss the issues in small groups. The final step was a full board discussion in which individual thoughts and small-group comments were shared. This kind of discussion takes time and energy, but it is an investment with the potential to yield good benefits to the board.

BOARD COMMITTEES AND THE HEAD OF SCHOOL

The Trustee Committee (sometimes called the Nominating Committee or Nominating and Board Development Committee) is the board's most important committee because it determines who sits on the board. The head of school should be an integral member of this committee. The head alone should not determine who joins the board, but he or she should have involvement and influence. As a Trustee Committee member, the head has an equal voice and can often offer unique perspectives on possible candidates. He or she should also have veto power over board nominations. After explaining the objection to a certain candidate — describing factors or experiences that cause the head to believe that it would be a serious mistake to ask John or Jane to join the board — the head's recommendation should hold. The Trustee Committee should respect this gravitas, and heads should use it sparingly.

The Trustee Committee also selects the head's professional partner, the chair of the board, typically recommending this appointment to the full board for approval. As Peter Cowen, head of the Pingree School in Massachusetts, puts it, "Under the heading 'Obvious but True' comes the notion that the head should have substantial input into the selection of the board chair." Adds Dick Jung, former head of the Bullis School in Maryland: "So often, the head of school and board chair relationship is both the predictor for and barometer of a thriving independent school. That relationship, therefore, deserves special cultivation from the very beginning."

Given the importance of this relationship, the head of school should have the most input into selecting the board chair. The head of school should not be the only person heard, but he or she should be an ex-officio member of the Nominating Committee, and candid discussions about potential chairs can take place in that context. The head should be given the opportunity to explain why this or that candidate would best help move the school forward and would be helpful to the head as well.

The head should play a key role in selecting the chair, but other voices need to be heard, too. An example comes from the John Burroughs School in Missouri. "We have the Nominating Committee chair, who is always the past president (chair), poll the past two or three presidents (chairs) for suggestions for a president-elect (chair-elect)," says Keith Shahan, head of school. "The Nominating Committee chair also consults with me during this process and then takes one or more names to the Nominating Committee."

SUPPORTING THE HEAD

It's obvious that a new head needs support. He or she is expected to arrive running at full speed (and get faster as the year progresses!). But the challenges and need for support don't end after the first year. Heads often confront a major challenge between their third and fifth year at a school. While challenges in the job always abound, this period of time can be more crucial because it is typically when the key leaders who selected the head — the members of the Search Committee — will leave the board. This means that the board has lost the leadership of those who were privy to the quiet challenges, those who researched the candidates and talked with the search consultants, and those who knew all the candidates (including the final candidate) best. It may be (indeed, should be) that an appreciation for the head and his or her role is pervasive among board members; sometimes, though, this is not the case. The following two suggestions, both related to committees, can decrease the chances that this problem will occur.

First, it helps to establish a Head Evaluation Committee, which should evaluate the head of school on an annual basis. Various evaluation formats and procedures exist, and all can yield good data about the head's performance, strengths, and weaknesses. The evaluation of a head of school should not be a parent referendum, nor should it be arbitrary. All evaluations should focus as objectively as possible on the head's goals (and, often, the goals for the school). Regardless of the evaluation model that is used, it's essential that the head work closely with the Evaluation Committee and feel comfortable with the approach that is chosen.

The format used in evaluating the head will evolve with the head's tenure at a school. It is natural and appropriate for a relatively new head to be evaluated differently than a head who is completing his or her 10th or 20th year at a school. The goals are the same — identifying areas warranting praise and areas needing improvement — but the procedures will vary. In all cases, the head's evaluation should focus on helping him or her improve performance. An ongoing Evaluation Committee not only helps a head grow; it also helps avoid surprises at contract-renewal time. If the head of school is not performing a satisfactory job, it is the board's responsibility to gracefully end the relationship and seek a replacement. If the head is doing a satisfactory job, it is the board's responsibility to support the head both privately and publicly.

Second, I would be most remiss if I failed to point out that there should not be an Education Committee of the board. The head of school, working with the faculty, provides the necessary educational leadership and acumen. If the board feels that additional educational insights or expertise are needed, this can be accomplished in a variety of ways without forming an Education Committee. The presence of such a committee, usually composed of caring and well-meaning board members and parents who are not trained as educators, is a formula for mischief. One head refers to his board's Education Committee as the "Second Guess Committee" because "that's what it continually does to me." At times, this kind of committee can become a sounding board for disgruntled faculty members or a back door to influence policy.

A key consideration in supporting the head is for board members to remember their roles and use appropriate chains of communication. Like the head, they represent the school at all times. It's tempting for board members to want to be problem-solvers; indeed, they should help address the board's challenges. That is different, however, from solving problems that properly belong to the head of school. It's essential that board members respect the organization's roles and boundaries, and it is the responsibility of the board chair — along with the members of the governance committee and the head — to provide the ongoing board training and awareness that enable this to happen.

THE HEAD'S JOB SATISFACTION

Job satisfaction, according to psychologist Frederick Herzberg, can be depicted on two parallel lines but not on a continuum. "Satisfiers," Herzberg says, are those factors that contribute to unhappiness if they are absent. Unsafe or uncomfortable working conditions or a lack of compensation makes it hard to feel good about your job, yet a nicer office or larger salary will not ultimately increase job satisfaction. Being paid more will enable the acquisition of more creature comforts but will not change the satisfaction that is derived from a job. Job satisfaction comes from "motivators." These are related to the job itself: How interesting is it? Is success attainable? Can it be varied and creative? Support begins with the board compensating the head of school competitively, so that the salary does not represent a distraction or disappointment. (Guidelines for administrative salary ranges are available at *www.nais.org*. Go to *www.nais.org* and type in "compensation" in the Quick Search box.)

Once a fair level of remuneration is achieved, boards must support heads by asking and by listening. The first ask — posed by the board chair to the head of school at the opening board meeting — might be, "How can we help you?" The question is powerful and the tone is rich. The subsequent dialogue will benefit everyone. Too often, a head of school is taken for granted. That may be inevitable, especially with long-standing and competent heads, so one of the board's priorities should be to express that appreciation. Board members, both individually and collectively, need to periodically say to the head, "You're working too late. Why don't you try to leave earlier a day or two each week?" They need to ask, "Are you using all your vacation days?" It is also common now for boards to offer heads membership in a health club. In all these ways, the board is asking, "How can we help you; what can we do?" Board members should remember that the job is too big for any one person to do alone.

Board members should listen to the head of school when he or she talks about a personal vision for the school and explains what is needed to get there. They need to ask how they can contribute. And they need to go to the head of school if they have a question or complaint; they need to advise peers to do the same. This is not to suggest that board members should defer to heads; that wouldn't benefit anyone. Good board members also question, and good board members also complain. This can and should be done in a tone of support and collaboration, and it is the job of both the head and the board chair to make sure this happens.

SUMMARY

A school can be no better than its governance. A school with good governance — one in which board members play effective roles in making decisions and supporting the school — can have unlimited potential. A school with poor governance, however — one in which board members fail to support the head and hamper his or her effectiveness — is destined to mediocrity at best.

Good heads of school respect and appreciate the role of the board of trustees and understand their responsibility for governance. They appreciate that their job is not only to work with the board but to empower and support it. They form a partnership with the board chair and use the board as a resource. As with any important relationship, a major investment of time and energy is required.

CHAPTER 3

■

SCHOOL CULTURE

DIFFERENT SCHOOLS, DIFFERENT CULTURES

The fictional Adams School, founded in the early 19th century, abounds in tradition. The boys wear uniforms, and each day begins with the Pledge of Allegiance recited in unison at an assembly. Standardized testing is an integral part of the Adams experience, and the school's success is determined in large part by where its graduates matriculate. Teachers at Adams are acknowledged to be experts in their field and are expected to contact students' parents if problems arise.

The fictional Feldspar School dates back to the 1950s and is often referred to as "Little Broadway." Rather than requiring a certain score on an admission test, the school considers student auditions a major part of the application process. At every level, student performances are choreographed, vibrant, and crisp. The arts focus goes beyond the usual curricular areas. Students are likely to be learning regional songs of the Civil War era, looking at paintings from

Colonial America, and dancing to celebrate various cultures. Indeed, teachers of academic areas may feel a bit like second-class citizens at faculty meetings. Sometimes Feldspar teachers seem more like cheerleaders and directors, and communication between parents and teachers can be spotty.

The fictional Major School was founded in the late 1960s and retains much of the philosophy of those turbulent times. A casual appearance is the norm for both students and faculty members. Standardized testing is done rather reluctantly, and students often demonstrate their understanding through presentations and performances. The Major School prides itself on the racial diversity of its students and staff and pursues a wide range of demographics. Teachers are expected to contact students' parents on a regular basis.

Despite their striking differences, these three schools serve their students well. Each has a unique view of the graduates it produces, a set path to achieve goals, and an expectation about professionals' roles and relationships. One could make the same statement about the range of independent schools in every community: While the schools' mission statements vary, each is designed to inspire student growth and achievement. A school's mission is the starting point, and schools are successful because they possess a strong and vibrant culture.

MISSION VS. CULTURE

It is the missions of Adams, Feldspar, and Major, after all, that determine how their success is defined and pursued. The mission tells the role of standardized tests in the educational program, although the term "standardized tests" is likely not part of the mission statement. The mission establishes the relationship between teachers and students and between teachers and students' parents (as well as between teachers and administrators, along with administrators and students' parents), although these interactions are typically not described. The mission tells how students will probably dress, although it surely doesn't address clothing directly.

A school's mission sets out both the *what* and the *how* in general terms: what is sought and how it is to be attained. The mission is approved by the board of trustees and sets the tone for the school. But it is the school culture that determines how people behave and whether the mission truly comes to life. Adams, Feldspar, and Major are very different schools, and each is successful not only because of its mission but also because of its culture.

An institutional culture informs and guides us far more deeply and pervasively than does a mission statement. Although all the faculty members should be able to articulate a school's mission, this is often not the case. However, everyone feels and knows the school's culture on a daily basis. If you ask a teacher, "What's important in this school?" the answer will speak to some aspect of the school's culture. The response may also address the school's mission — indeed, the mission and culture should be congruent — but the answer will stem from the school's culture. People believe mission; they live culture.

We touch a school's culture every day; it affects our perceptions and our behaviors. In *Leading Change*, James O'Toole says, "Culture is the unique whole — the shared ideas, customs, assumptions, expectations, philosophy, traditions, mores, and values — that determines how a group of people will behave." In *Shaping School Culture*, Terrence Deal and Kent Peterson note that "Cultural patterns are highly enduring, have a powerful impact on performance, and shape the ways people think, act, and feel." Roland Barth says, "The school's culture dictates, in no uncertain terms, 'the way we do things around here.'" A school's culture tells people how they should behave.

FACULTY CULTURE

In many schools, a great deal of administrative attention and effort is given to forming and managing the aspects of a school's culture that relate to students. Questions that guide student behavior are announced, and the answers are promulgated and reinforced: What is appropriate student attire? How should students conduct themselves in the halls or at sporting events? What are the expectations for student behavior on weekends? Is there an honor code? Teachers and administrators exert great energy in creating a school culture that will channel students' expectations and energies in positive ways. They may say, "We're here for the students!" or "Students come first at the Pike School." All of this may be true, and we do need to channel students' behaviors, but thinking of school culture only as it pertains to students is a missed opportunity.

Why? Because a school's culture informs and guides everyone's behavior, not just that of the students. A school's culture provides a framework for educational decisions and practices. It determines pedagogy and student assessment as well as the nature of communication with students' parents and of faculty relationships. When a school culture is strong, faculty members approach problems and act in certain ways because "that's the way things are done here." There is an expectation and tone that almost guarantee a consistent approach by everyone; the way to proceed is clear.

Focusing on faculty culture means that the focus is also on student culture (whereas the converse is not the case). "Culture is defined by the habits and practices of teachers," says Andrew Wooden, head of the Bosque School in New Mexico. Because the faculty sets the tone and manages the expectations for student behavior, administrators must begin by focusing on the school culture as it relates to faculty members. They need to spend more time establishing the culture for faculty than for students. Of course, school heads should also give thought to a school's administrative culture. Just as teachers set the tone for students, administrators set the tone for teachers.

CREATING A CULTURE

Perhaps the most important task of a head of school is to embody and monitor the school's culture. Mary Worch, head of the Woods Academy in Maryland, offers her view: "School culture, I believe, is a living organism within a school. It can be very visible as well as strongly sensed by the school constituency and by visitors in the building. This experience is part of the 'essence' of a school. I believe that the culture comes from the top. At our school, we talk about it as the 'Woods way.'"

Without a strong culture, administrative edicts tend to govern behaviors —

or else there is no consistency or direction and teachers are on their own. In the latter case, teacher "freelancing" becomes the norm, which results in students' parents being far less confident about the quality of education their children will receive at the school. Parents want to know that the school's mission will be pursued even though the names and demographics of subsequent years' teachers will change. What this really means is that parents want the school's culture to remain consistent from year to year to year.

When a culture is strong, the ways to approach problems are obvious and consistent. A strong school culture can make administrators' jobs easier because they do not need to weigh in on every decision. The culture guides others' behavior whether or not an administrator is physically present. It guides teacher attitudes and behaviors on all issues, from how to respond to a dyspeptic parent to how to deal with a student who doesn't wish to try. The culture determines the degree to which teachers view their colleagues and administrators as resources.

Good leaders recognize that a strong culture doesn't just happen; it must be developed, reinforced, and reinforced some more. The school culture should be obvious from what is said and done by school leaders. Indeed, strong leaders seek and create opportunities to use the words or phrases that convey school culture.

Matthew Gould, head of the Community School in Missouri, takes this approach: "I repeat our school's two or three most important core values to every constituent every chance I get. I mention them at faculty meetings, board meetings, alumni meetings, and prospective parent meetings and with small and large groups of parents." A key point is the importance of using succinct statements: words and phrases that can be readily embraced and repeated. The payoff, in Gould's experience: "After several years here, other people are repeating those values and 'owning' them. People are repeating these core values as if they, themselves, thought them up. It's terrific, and that is the power of leadership. We, as heads of school, through our oral and written communication, can create a shared language in our schools."

As in so many other areas, the little things are the big things. A school may proclaim that everyone is equal, but what's the message when only the head of school has a designated parking space? The banner may say, "All students succeed here," but what's the message if the head of school asks only about the students who are the high flyers or checks only on those who struggle? The school may claim to value professional growth and faculty collegiality, but are these issues talked about with the faculty? Does the school budget include funds for professional development? What is done to encourage faculty sharing?

PRACTICING WHAT WE PREACH

There are many ways of teaching and reinforcing a school's culture. It is imperative that administrators, teachers, and support staff know what is valued at every turn. This begins at the top: Unless the head of school is clear and consistent, the messages can be mixed. That is not to say that teacher autonomy or creativity should be taken out of the equation but, rather, that the important aspects of culture must be reinforced. Krissa Bloom, an independent-school elementary school teacher, refers to schools having an "identity crisis" if this doesn't happen.

For example, I've yet to come across a school that does not claim to be a learning organization or tout how well its faculty learns with and from one another. This sounds good, but how is that brought to life? (Or *is* it brought to life?) Are times carved out of in-service days and planning sessions to enable teachers to plan together as colleagues? Do schedules exist that support multidisciplinary or cross-grade collaborations? Is faculty collegiality something that is addressed in teachers' end-of-year evaluations? Whether or not the school uses a performance pay plan, are teachers rewarded for taking the time to share their skills and work with others? What are the expectations for faculty members — and administrators, including the head of school — to serve on committees? How does the school draw on the expertise of senior faculty members? How does the mentor program support newer teachers?

Similarly, when faculty meetings are only about disseminating information, an opportunity is lost. In meetings with groups of teachers, administrators can reinforce the school's culture not just by what they say but by what they do. One-way meetings in which administrators talk and teachers listen are not a good use of anyone's time. If that much information needs to be shared, and sometimes it does, then it should be shared in writing, and the meeting time should be used for clarifications and questions. The same principles we use for motivating and reaching our students apply to motivating and reaching our faculty. Irrespective of age, learning takes place when learners are motivated and engaged, and that's more difficult when you're only an audience member.

Further, how can we really believe we have a learning organization if learning doesn't take place at faculty meetings? Time is our most precious resource, so by devoting time to learning, we make a very salient statement about our school's culture — and our role. Think of the rich discussions that would emerge and the powerful lessons that would be reinforced if 15 minutes were allocated at the start of each faculty meeting for responding to the sorts of questions that are listed in the sidebar below.

The opportunity to respond to these types of questions and share their thoughts with others just might cause teachers to look forward to attending faculty meetings! The specific questions are less important than the fact that they are asked and ample time is allotted for them to be discussed. Doing this shows that administrators value reflection and professional growth.

AWAKEN YOUR FACULTY MEETINGS: QUESTIONS FOR FACULTY DISCUSSION

- What have you done in the past week that makes you proud?
- What have you done in the past week that you'd do differently if you had the opportunity?
- What curriculum areas should we delete or de-emphasize?
- What is frustrating you?
- Who has been helpful to you in the past week?
- How can the administration help you become a better teacher?

Asking questions also gives us a chance to reinforce our values. At a recent faculty meeting, I spent about 25 minutes pursuing the issue of "joyful learning." I began by asking teachers to think a minute or two about some joyful learning experiences that had taken place in their classrooms; then I had them meet in small groups and share with others.

Another strategy would be to convene a faculty Question Committee, whose members would meet monthly and create the questions for faculty meetings and help lead the discussion. Here again, not only is the process rich and beneficial, but it also affirms the culture of our schools.

CULTURE AFFECTS EVERYONE

A school's culture influences all the members of a school community, not just the faculty. How students' parents view annual giving is informed by the school culture, for example. Is it assumed that the school's fiscal needs have merit and that parents should donate as much as they are able? Or do the school's pleas for funds ring hollow, resulting in a disappointing percentage of donors? The school culture is a big factor in this formula. Indeed, school heads, development directors, and annual giving chairs spend much time trying to influence the culture of giving.

This means that school heads also need to give thought to parent communication with culture in mind. School communications should do more than convey upcoming events; they are opportunities to shape culture. For example, giving precious space in a newsletter to share a story about a student who reached out to help others, instead of limiting coverage to winning teams or National Merit Finalists, is a statement about school culture. Parent communications are an opportunity to teach and reinforce a school's mission and values. John Delautre, head of the St. Francis School in Kentucky, speaks to the value of a consistent message for all constituents: "The importance of consistency in the way things are done throughout the institution is something I try to keep in front of me at all times." A school's culture frames the perceptions and thinking of every member of the organization.

This point on the pervasiveness and power of culture is made in a story that Tom Peters, the co-author of *In Search of Excellence*, shared years ago. There was one Honda dealership that excelled in customer loyalty among all the Honda dealerships in Los Angeles. The people who used this dealership raved about the quality of its vehicles. In trying to ascertain why this was the case, Honda of Japan determined that it wasn't due to the actual automobiles; the Hondas sold at this dealership were no different from the Hondas sold at any of the other dealers in Los Angeles. But customers talked about how much they loved their Hondas, how these were the best cars they'd ever driven, and how they would definitely recommend a Honda to a friend. When they were asked why this was the case, customer after customer talked about the friendly welcome they received from the receptionist, bookkeeper, or service manager. "They asked about my children," a customer would say, or "They always took the time to hear my concerns." Few people talked about the actual virtues of the Honda, despite their stated loyalty to the car.

I found this to be a striking message about the power of the culture of that Honda dealership. People bought their vehicles there not simply because of the Honda — Los Angeles has many Honda dealerships — but because of how they were treated. The culture of the dealership said, "Customers are important, and we need to focus on them." That's very different from a culture that says, "Profit is what we're about." Profit will follow loyalty, and that comes from a culture that respects the customer. Re-enrollments and successful fund raising will follow from that kind of culture, too.

As John Delautre points out, a school's culture is conveyed in myriad ways, some obvious and others less so. Often the things we take for granted speak volumes about our school's culture; this includes the messages that are — and are not — displayed in our halls and on our walls. Walking through the school at midnight, one should be able to tell what is valued and which kinds of students succeed. If the culture is touted as a learning organization, one in which everyone grows, that should be obvious, too. Paul Geise of Pine Point School in Connecticut posts the mission statement throughout the school in various public spaces so that it is overtly expressed again and again. Like Matthew Gould, Geise says, "I have repeatedly used the key phrases within our mission statement in nearly every public talk, every letter, and every article that I have written. It has become something of a vehicle for ribbing me that I use these phrases unabatedly." Establishing the culture — teaching it — is too important to be left to chance. A strong school culture helps determine the context in which behaviors are seen and, thus, perceived.

Often an act or practice can be perceived in radically dissimilar ways. For example, is the long carpool line a commentary about valuing efficiency and safety, or is it a statement about offering limited parent access to the building? Does providing teachers' home phone numbers demonstrate that faculty members are receptive to questions or concerns, or does it indicate that they need to respond to parents' whims? These questions are answered within the context of the school culture. If a culture is strong, the perceptions that work against it will be ignored and discarded; they are viewed as exceptions and aberrations. If a culture is not strong, however, the range of perceptions and interpretations may know no bounds. Indeed, one of the reasons effective school leaders continually educate everyone about their school's culture is that it serves as a framework through which experiences are viewed. The culture defines reality and becomes self-reinforcing.

In describing the power of school culture, I noted that it needs to be both strong and vibrant. By strong, I refer to the pervasiveness and consistency of the culture. Is what is valued at the school clear to everyone? If not, a primary job of the head of school is to clarify and communicate these values at school-wide assemblies, in publications, in small-group meetings, and in one-on-one conversations — quite simply, everywhere.

And by vibrant, I mean that even a strong culture should evolve. While values may remain constant, cultures can change to reflect the changing landscape, the mission of the school, or both. Of course, this can be much harder when the head of school has held the position for a significant amount of time. Rita Bornstein's work on college presidents is relevant. In *Legitimacy in the Academic Presidency*, she notes that "Virtually every organization is prisoner to 'the way we do things here.' Often it takes new leadership to ask, 'Why are we doing things this way?'"

Cultures change slowly. For example, a school known for its rigorous admissions standards may decide to become more inclusive and accept students with greater academic needs. If that decision is reflected in the school culture, everyone can succeed. But if the culture remains the same, that decision changes only which students walk through the door and not who will succeed; the mission becomes mere rhetoric. Again, it may take a new head of school — or one who is very thoughtful about change and willing to pay the price that accompanies it — to keep the culture vibrant.

NEW HEADS

As noted, changing the culture of a school can be easier with the arrival of a new head of school, one who is not shackled by many years at the same desk in the same office with the same relationships in the same school. The new head, after all, was selected for certain qualities, and surely the ability to improve the school (no matter how good it already is) was an important factor in his or her selection. In a sense, then, the new head has a bit of license to question old beliefs and practices. As with so many other issues of leadership, communication is the key. Changing others' behavior is never easy, and it's even harder if the logic for the change is not shared. Without a rationale, it's only natural for others to fall behind the shield of "We've always done it this way," implying (or even stating), "We're doing just fine, thank you very much." Collaboratively defining the problems — the opportunities — so that everyone can see the need to change is essential.

Too often, however, school leaders are so busy seeking what they know is must-needed change that they fail to take the time to listen. Writing in the August 19, 2007, *Wall Street Journal*, Carol Hymowitz notes that "Generally, employees are more likely to support a CEO pushing strategic change if he or she doesn't at the same time run roughshod over their culture. Yet few new

CEOs take the time to learn about the culture they have inherited."

An important distinction is whether the new head was an internal or external candidate. Years ago, in studying the selection of public school superintendents, Richard Carlson used the terms "place centered" and "career centered" to distinguish between them. As we might infer, superintendents who were "place centered" were those selected from within the district, whereas "career centered" superintendents were chosen from the outside. Carlson's finding was that the decision about whether to choose a career-centered or place-centered superintendent reflected the board's desire for change. If the board was pleased with the status of the school district, the choice of a place-centered superintendent would follow. If, however, there was a desire for change, a career-centered superintendent would likely be selected. That same logic often applies to the decision of a board of trustees about whether to select an internal or external candidate to be the new head of school.

As such, it can be much more difficult for the new head who was an internal candidate to change a school's culture. The expectation for the head is largely that things will continue as usual. Unless the internal candidate who is now the head of school moves carefully in changing culture, he or she can be perceived as inconsistent or, even, hypocritical. Even if the head were not to challenge or change the culture, the mere fact that his or her role changes means that relationships with colleagues must change, too. These are not insurmountable barriers, but the new head needs to be aware of the cost and thoughtfully plan how to proceed. "What are the issues, and who are my allies?" are questions that must be asked again and again, as the allies will change with the issues.

In contrast, when a new head who is an outsider takes over, especially if an internal candidate (or candidates) also applied for the job, there is an anticipation that the head will change things. Everything is, or seems to be, in flux. How long is the honeymoon? Here's Bornstein again: "As soon as the new president begins to act, his or her initial legitimacy is threatened as a period of scrutiny and testing begins." These are not insurmountable barriers either, but the new head also needs to be aware of the cost and thoughtfully plan how to proceed. "What are the issues, and who are my allies?" must again be asked.

There is legitimate disagreement about how quickly a new head of school should move to change a school and its culture. Some believe that the new head should move slowly at first, after establishing trusting relationships. Others say that the new head should act swiftly while he or she still has the endorsement of the search committee and the support of the board. In truth, the correct answer will vary by school and by circumstance. I believe that all new heads have a unique opportunity to question assumptions and cause others to reflect on philosophies and procedures. This window closes quickly, though, and newly formed trusting relationships can sometimes make the job even harder.

YOUR SCHOOL'S CULTURE

Sometimes, like the fish who presumably isn't aware of the water in which it lives, a head of school can fail to see his or her own school's culture. Maybe the head has been at the school long enough that things just "seem to be"; maybe he or she is fairly new and hasn't grasped the relationships and history. Or perhaps the head sees the culture differently than the faculty does. Doing a culture inventory reveals the implicit assumptions and highlights the disparities that may exist in how aspects of the school are perceived. (NAIS has an online school climate survey that can help. To access, go to *www.nais.org* and click on Assessment of Inclusivity and Multiculturalism (AIM).)

What about your school? As a first step, answering the questions in the sidebar on the next page (inspired by Roland Barth) can provide insight into your school's culture. Because perception is reality, you may wish to ask others to answer the questions and then compare your responses. The collegiality that can stem from this kind of dialogue is powerful. If a school's culture is strong, there will be near unanimity in responses, regardless of the organizational roles people occupy. If a culture is not strong, there will be a range of opinions, some quite contradictory to others. And if teachers and administrators vary in responses, chances are that the teachers are correct in identifying the true school culture.

DEFINING OUR SCHOOL'S CULTURE

- What qualities does the school seek in hiring faculty members?
- What criteria are used in evaluating teachers?
- What qualities do the administrators value most in teachers?
- What is the purpose of faculty meetings?
- What determines which students are accepted at the school?
- On what basis are students assigned to classrooms?
- What is done for students who struggle?
- What is done for students who excel?
- What is the relationship between faculty members and students' parents?
- What happens if a big donor complains about something?
- What should we be celebrating?

SUMMARY

Great schools have powerful cultures. To this end, an integral task of every head is to be thoughtful about his or her school's culture and to consciously use it to guide attitudes and actions.

When a school's culture is taken into consideration, as it must be, every question becomes a bit contextual. That is, although all decisions should be driven by what is educationally sound and good, school leaders also need to consider the political implications and costs of their decisions. It is naive not to do so. Heads should ask themselves and their colleagues, "Is there a way to get everyone on board? Can there be compromises that don't lower the quality but result in consensus? How will this decision affect the culture?" Good school leaders ponder all of these aspects, recognizing that it's not sufficient to be right. Everyone — students and faculty alike — benefits from good decisions.

When we are thinking about context and leverage points, it's important to recognize that the faculty culture sets the tone for everyone. It may help to think of the school as a series of concentric circles, beginning with the head of school as the center figure. Then, moving outward, there is the administrative team, then the faculty, then the support staff, followed by students and their parents. Each inner circle influences all those beyond it. Thus, focusing on the faculty culture will affect the student culture, focusing on students affects their parents, and so on. It may be harder to focus on faculty culture than on students, but this is too important an area to ignore. Administrators should begin with the innermost circle, questioning and considering their own assumptions, and then do so for their administrative team.

CHAPTER 4

■

TEACHER GROWTH AND DEVELOPMENT

THE ONLY CONSTANT IS CHANGE

When I talk with other school administrators, whether it's over a cup of coffee at Kayak's Cafe, at a conference, or during a break at a presentation I'm making, the issue of change often comes up. More accurately, the issue of resistance to change comes up. It doesn't take long for someone to mention how difficult it is to get the faculty to go from here to there or how hard it is to help this teacher reflect on her performance or to get that teacher to engage in a different sort of behavior. Sometimes the discussion is about helping students' parents see things differently and change their behaviors. Occasionally it's about how hard it is for us to change. The ability to manage change is one of the most challenging parts of our jobs, and it's also one of the most integral to our success.

"Why is it so hard for people to change?" I often wonder. In every setting, including my own, some people cling to what has worked in the past. (I know this is true of me occasionally as well.) They have an effective strategy that works for them and just aren't interested in exploring anything that's different. The fact that the new idea or different practice might be an improvement doesn't persuade them. Their assumption is that what worked well yesterday will work just as well today and tomorrow. That thinking, though, is naive at best. Neither organizations nor individuals stand still; they — we — either grow or decline. (What's worse, of course, is when people cling to what has *not* worked in the past. The good news is that bringing about change may be easier in these situations because the lack of effectiveness mandates doing something different, despite and over objections.)

There are four kinds of thinking that cause people to resist change. Opposition to new ideas and practices often stems from several, or all, of these factors, and thinking about them can help us determine how to respond and proceed. And respond and proceed we must. When presented with a new initiative, the naysayers think (and sometimes reply) with one or more of the following:

- "I don't need to listen to you."
- "We're already doing too much."
- "We're already doing just fine."
- "I already have the answer."

"I don't need to listen to you." Perhaps, more properly, this is phrased as "Who are you???" because one question mark may not suffice in conveying the sense of indignation or the recusant attitude. This question, whether formally asked or, more likely, simply thought, addresses the credibility of the person initiating the change: Does the school head have enough knowledge or experience? Does he or she know our school? Does he or she know me? (In schools with frequent administrative turnover, "Who are you?" is often followed by "I was here before you came and I'll be here after you're gone.")

It can be tempting to respond to this sort of question and attitude by leaning on one's hierarchical position; after all, the head of school is in charge, right? Well, yes and no. School leaders can run into difficulties when they rely too much on their position and title as they try to bring about change. This is even more pronounced when the leader is new to the organization (and exacerbated if the leader is new to the leadership role). Writing in the January 2007 *Harvard Business Review*, Linda Hill notes, "New managers soon learn, however, that when direct reports are told to do something, they don't necessarily respond. In fact, the more talented the subordinate, the less likely he or she is to simply follow orders." Hill continues, "Many new managers are surprised by how difficult it is to earn people's respect and trust. They are shocked, and even insulted, that their expertise and track record don't speak for themselves." Similarly, in *The Art of School Leadership*, I wrote, "A generation ago, a boss could expect an employee to do something just because he told him to do it. Today, employee acceptance and compliance are not based on the positional, legitimate power that bosses hold." Simply because the board of trustees has anointed Mary as the leader of the school doesn't mean the faculty will defer to her or trust her judgment.

So what's a head of school to do? In *Good to Great and the Social Sectors*, Jim Collins contrasts the differences between executive and legislative leaders. The executive leader simply makes the decision, period, and everyone goes along with it. This attitude would more likely be the case in a privately held company or family business (but even there, this approach has its limitations). Legislative leadership, by contrast, stresses the importance of consensus. "No individual leader — not even the nominal chief executive — has enough structural power to make the most important decisions by himself or herself," Collins says. "Legislative leadership relies more upon persuasion, political currency, and shared interests to create the conditions for the right decision to happen." This means that school leaders cannot mandate or command if they want to bring about lasting and meaningful change. Leaders must take the time to know their employees and establish credibility.

Similarly, writing in *Scientific American Mind*, Stephen Reicher, Michael Platow, and Alexander Haslam note that "Effective leaders must work to understand the values and opinions of their followers — rather than assuming absolute authority — to enable a productive dialogue with followers about what the group embodies and stands for and thus how it should act." Rita Bornstein observes that "To be seen as competent leaders and managers, presidents must demonstrate a willingness to communicate, collaborate, and consult with all constituents and value the shared governance system for its democratic distribution of decision-making among expert groups."

Collins notes, "The best leaders of the future — in the social sectors and business — will not be purely executive or legislative; they will have a knack for knowing when to play their executive chips and when not to." Even in those times when the leader cashes in executive chips — which should be rare — it must be done carefully. The worst approach is to simply say, "I'm in charge and this is my decision." That may or may not elicit compliance, but it will definitely elicit resentment. It's better to say, "I'm in charge, this is the decision, and here's my rationale." Even though leaders may think it's terribly obvious why they chose this particular path, they need to take the time to share their thinking. Doing so often results in positive feelings, even when the listener already knew the rationale. The best approach is, "I'm in charge, I've listened to you and gathered information, and I understand that no solution will please everyone. Nonetheless, I've determined — again, with your help, thank you — how we will proceed. Here's the plan and here's my rationale." Even this approach should be taken infrequently and carefully, however. For school leaders to remind employees that they are the boss is the quickest way to incur resistance. Resorting to one's formal authority too often ultimately narrows and weakens power.

"We're already doing too much." This is a comment I hear often, and with good reason. My teachers *are* doing too much, and I'm sure yours are, too. We have added more and more responsibilities to teachers' roles and increased our expectations of their performance. Expectations of teachers in independent schools have increased in other ways, too. As the costs of tuition have risen and the available pool of students has decreased, we all find ourselves spending much more time on marketing our schools. Teachers feel that pinch and pressure, too. At my school, for example, we have added a Saturday open house for prospective parents, and we focus more on parents' experiences and perceptions as they tour our building. Each of these strategies relies on teacher skills, and each demands additional teacher energy.

The solution to "we're already doing too much" is taking stock of what we are presently doing and then reducing or eliminating some activities. This is far easier said than done, but it needs to happen. Doing this with faculty members increases their awareness of the tensions and challenges that school leaders are trying to address, and that is always helpful. A few years ago, I formed a Balance Committee at my school, made up of teachers and administrators. Our task was to examine the competing demands on our time and try to find a way to achieve a healthy educational and personal balance. We didn't solve the problem, but everyone came away with a greater appreciation for the inherent tensions resulting from the philosophy of our school. (Alas, the fact that I'm considering convening another Balance Committee illustrates the difficulties surrounding this issue.)

"We're already doing just fine." It can be hard to argue for change when students come into our school smiling each morning, when they perform well on standardized tests, and when they matriculate to fine schools. But these positive indicators, while wonderful, are not sufficient. The world is changing around us, and the old forms of education and preparation need to change, too. In five very different books — *The World Is Flat*; *A Whole New Mind*; *China, Inc.*; *The Long Tail*; and *Five Minds for the Future* — the authors paint visions of tomorrow's economically interconnected and far more demanding world in which creative problem-solving abilities will be even more important. In *The Long Emergency*, John Kunstler argues that the inevitable worldwide energy shortage will render skyscrapers, interstate commerce, and oil-powered machines useless.

Some of these changes are already in front of us. The Internet is less than 15 years old, for example, yet it has already had a profound impact on information and learning. It took the St. Louis Public Library 135 years to acquire its four and a half million holdings, while the Internet adds that many new documents every three days. We know more about how children learn than ever before, and each bit of new knowledge leads to even more discoveries. Societies and organizations are changing, and while we can argue about whether the changes are positive or negative, the changes will occur. Simply performing well on standardized tests and gaining access to other good schools, important as these outcomes are, will not prepare students adequately for the future.

So while we may be doing fine today (and we should take the time to applaud that fact), it's necessary to determine what's needed in order to do fine tomorrow. An important piece of school leadership, then, is helping everyone — faculty and staff, students and their parents, the community, and the board of trustees — look at the possibilities for tomorrow and plan what needs to be done to help today's students succeed. Regardless of the predictions, it will be clear that we need to do more and we need to do it differently. At that point, everyone's response, not just that of the head of school, will become "Yes, we're doing fine, but that's not enough."

A danger here is that by focusing on the large-scale issues, we may fail to give attention to the everyday behaviors that continue to make the difference. We can have meeting after meeting about whether we should add Mandarin Chinese to our curriculum or how to weave community service into our students' experiences, but we can't neglect to make that phone call to a parent or forget to teach basic algebra. In *The Starbucks Experience*, Joseph Michelli notes this tension when he says, "The trick for management, therefore, is to get employees to see the bigger picture."

"I already have the answer." This attitude is based on how an individual views himself or herself. Simply put, it is the difference between past tense and present tense, between having learned and being a learner. In a perfect world, we would all continue to be learners, and each day would be ripe with discovery. In fact, there is a tendency to continue on the path that has been successful. We all have finite energy and finite time, so it's natural to want to stay with what works. If this is the case, the strategies outlined above are appropriate.

All too often, though, this sort of attitude is due to a reluctance to take risks. After all, trying something new means increasing the likelihood of failure, and people vary a great deal in their willingness to do this. Carol Dweck, in *Mindset*, describes two mindsets about intelligence, "fixed" and "growth," and says that our willingness to tolerate risk is determined by which view we embrace.

Those who believe in the fixed mindset (whether or not they are aware of it) feel that their intelligence is finite and therefore that they must avoid failure. She calls this "an urgency to prove yourself over and over." The opposite of this is the growth mindset, a belief that "your basic qualities are things you can cultivate through your efforts." The emphasis is on developing yourself, as opposed to validating yourself. The implications of this are quite powerful: "The passion for stretching yourself and sticking to it, even (or especially) when it's not going well, is the hallmark of the growth mindset." Dweck says that "People in a growth mindset don't just seek challenge, they thrive on it" and cites sociologist Benjamin Barber: "I don't divide the world into the weak or strong, or the successes and the failures.... I divide the world into learners and non-learners."

People with a fixed mindset, who seek the safe and predictable, are most likely to rely on "I already have the answer." When leaders encounter people with this attitude — and they are at all of our schools playing all kinds of roles, including, no doubt, the head of school in some places — the solution is education. First, it's important to formally address the notion of mindset. One approach is to have a faculty group read Dweck's book and discuss its implications. (Our faculty did this one summer, and it became a frequent topic at faculty meetings.) Another approach is for the head to read and share, using the information to elicit discussion at faculty meetings. Once this is done, school leaders must consciously work to create an environment in which risk-taking is promoted and the logical consequences — failures — are not just tolerated but understood and accepted. *The goal is not to avoid errors but to learn from them*: The Make New Mistakes philosophy sets the stage for collegiality and personal growth. When this happens, "I already have the answer" becomes a starting point for growth, not the end of the investigation.

TEACHER EVOLUTION

What are the differences between a teacher with three years' experience and one with 13 or 23 years in the classroom? While every generalization has exceptions, it's fair to note that teachers' careers evolve along a somewhat predictable path through certain phases. After all, growth is growth, whether the individual growing is 8, 18, or 38 years old. Growth is sequential (we crawl before we walk, and we walk before we run), and growth is developmental (we learn when we are ready).

All the models of teacher evolution share some biases. With greater experience, teachers gain more knowledge and often assume a wider level of engagement and responsibility within the school. That is fairly predictable. These stages are compounded, of course, by the fact that teachers' careers do not take place in a vacuum. As a teacher's status moves from new teacher to veteran over the years, the size and complexity of his or her family often change. As teachers age, their health and that of their loved ones become an issue. Changing roles at home and in life certainly have an impact on the roles teachers choose to assume at school.

I see teachers evolving through four roles. How long a teacher remains in any role will vary; what will not vary is that the roles are sequential (see sidebar on the next page).

In my own investigation of the roles through which teachers pass, I convened a group of senior teachers at New City School, each with at least a decade of experience (and most with more than 20 years of teaching experience).

TEACHERS' ROLES

1. **Novice.** This period is typically during a teacher's first two years in the classroom. The teacher has technical training and enthusiasm but lacks experience and wisdom. He or she is fully occupied in teaching, planning, and grading, working more hours than anticipated. The teacher may question whether or not this is the right profession.

2. **Craftsman.** With a few years of success, the teacher has the knowledge and skills necessary to allow him or her to reach students. Rather than easing the task, however, the additional expertise means that the teacher is more aware of students' needs. Job satisfaction may increase, but so may frustration. The teacher still works longer than he or she would like but accepts this as part of the job.

3. **Professional.** Understanding what is and is not possible enables the teacher to continue to improve while, at the same time, working to make a difference in other aspects of the school. The teacher begins to look outside the classroom to make a difference in schoolwide (or even broader) endeavors. Mentoring others, perhaps including administrators, seems like a natural part of the teacher's role. Writing on the NAIS website, Pat Bassett says, "Mid-career teachers run the show; pay attention to what they say and how they operate (and on a bad day, stay clear, because often life is tough for them)."

4. **Senior.** Retirement is not that far away, and while the teacher still works hard, it's clear that a piece of his or her heart and head has changed. The teacher may be far more interested in pursuits beyond the classroom, whether mentoring and leaving a legacy or simply looking forward to the opportunity to sleep later and not grade papers. Particularly in schools where the energy level is high and new ideas are embraced, it's important that senior teachers feel appreciated and respected. Bassett terms these faculty members "an invaluable resource."

I proposed these career stages to them and asked how their needs were different now than after their fifth year of teaching. Universally, they talked about how their needs were much the same as after year five. "I still need feedback, someone to push me forward," said one teacher, and another responded, "We still know we don't have the answers." They all mentioned having a vested interest in our school and being interested in and responsible for things that happened outside their classroom. All echoed a desire to learn with and from their colleagues and to mentor others. In talking about working with newer teachers, they said:

- "New teachers need help in filtering. I used to say 'yes' to everything."
- "I want to share what I have learned."
- "It's important to know that it's okay to do less."
- "I used to be intimidated dealing with my students' parents."
- "I can be a resource."
- "There's no reason for them to make the same mistakes I made."

I asked these senior teachers what we, the administration, could do for them. A quick reply was "This kind of meeting is good. We want a chance to talk about it, whatever the 'it' is." Everyone agreed that convening this sort of group on a regular basis, with or without an agenda, would be worthwhile. I left the meeting appreciative of their time and vowing to do this again. Subsequently, I formed a Seasoned Teachers Committee, composed of teachers with 15 or more years of experience at New City School. The group meets regularly with me to exchange ideas and offer suggestions.

SUMMARY

Vibrant teacher growth and development are essential if a school is to flourish. Teacher growth must be continuous, relevant, and interesting: We should apply the same standards to teachers' growth that we do to the growth of their students! However excellent a faculty is today, it must be better tomorrow and better still next year. That is a daunting challenge, to be sure. However, if it is doable — and it must be doable — the solution lies in creating a mindset that supports growth.

School leaders must make teacher development a major priority for themselves and their board of trustees. A focus on teacher growth must be evident in the school schedule, in the planning and organizing of faculty meetings, throughout professional development, and in the budget.

CHAPTER 5

■

FACULTY COLLEGIALITY

THE COLLEGIALITY CHALLENGE

What's the most important factor in determining whether a school is a setting in which children grow and learn? It's not the number of computers available, nor is it a low pupil-teacher ratio, although those factors are certainly important. It's not even how well the faculty is paid, even though hiring excellent teachers and paying them well are essential. In fact, the most important factor in determining whether a school is a setting in which children grow and learn is whether the school is a setting in which adults grow and learn.

The key to success in any organization is having employees who continue to learn and grow, yet too often this is not a priority for leaders. Indeed, "Does your organization have a learning disability?" is a question posed by Peter Senge in his book *The Fifth Discipline*. He says, "It is no accident that most organizations learn poorly. The way they are designed and managed, the way people's jobs are defined, and, most importantly, the way we have all been taught to think and interact (not only in organizations but more broadly) create fundamental learning disabilities."

Strangely and sadly, this lack of appreciation and understanding about the importance of adult learning is true even in education. If any settings should evince learning among employees, it is schools, yet often they don't. In retrospect, the lack of focus on adult learning is a logical consequence of the way we have defined schools. To begin with, school buildings were designed to enable the supervision and orderly movement of students. The egg-carton model of school architecture and organization prevails even today. Individual classrooms are adjacent to one another with parallel doors facing a hall (not unlike prison cellblocks).

In a school building that contains 100,000 square feet and dozens of teachers, the faculty lounge can be one of the smaller rooms, and even that tiny space may be intruded upon by refrigerators and copying machines. Years ago, I was involved in designing a new school that was to be based on Howard Gardner's theory of multiple intelligences. The first meeting began with the architects asking whether one room should be devoted to each of the eight intelligences (the answer was no), but it had not occurred to them to create a space for faculty meetings and collaboration. A principal who was involved in the design of a new school once told me that his plea for a larger teachers' lounge was greeted with "That's a waste of good space."

The conditions that deter faculty collaboration are often exacerbated in secondary schools, which are organized by academic departments or curricular areas. The social studies department is located and works apart from the mathematics department, which is down the hall and works separately from the fine arts department, and so on. Occasionally, some teachers move from classroom to classroom during the day, without having a home base or desk they can call their own. Administrators' offices are small spaces with access often guarded zealously by a secretary who serves the same function as a crocodile in a moat. Collaboration may still occur, but these conditions make it more difficult for faculty members to learn and grow together.

The biggest obstacle to collaboration, however, is neither the architectural design of schools nor teachers' schedules. The major hurdle is the history and ethos of the teaching profession. "Teaching is a very autonomous experience," says Sara Lawrence Lightfoot, author of *The Good High School*. "But the flip side of autonomy is that teachers experience loneliness and isolation." In too many schools, teachers close their classroom door and spend the majority of their working hours with children, only talking hurriedly with other adults over a break, during lunch, or while standing at the copy machine. This is not terribly surprising since many educators chose to enter the profession to work with students, not with other adults. (Indeed, sometimes the teachers who work best with their students are those who have the most difficulty working with their colleagues, their students' parents, or administrators.)

In all fairness, until recently, the need for teachers to collaborate wasn't seen as particularly important. For many years, successful teachers drew information and content from teachers' guides and their academic preparation and presented material to rows of students. Teaching consisted of transferring skills and knowledge. This may have been even truer at independent schools that enrolled only advantaged children who came to school ready to learn.

Fortunately, today our profession embraces far more progressive views about how students learn. From constructivism to problem-based learning to multiple intelligences to service learning, we have become much more aware that students learn best when they are engaged, when instruction is developmental, and when learning is relevant. We have not, though, transferred that awareness to how adults learn. "The problems and challenges in the workplaces of the 21st century are impossible to solve alone. That's one reason why teamwork is now the dominant mode of work nearly everywhere — except in education," notes Tony Wagner in *Phi Delta Kappan.*

Virtually every school administrator would agree that teachers should be learning and growing. After all, faculty members spend countless hours in meetings, in-service and professional development sessions, and conferences and workshops. This is all well and good, but it is not enough. Too often when learning occurs, it's done in isolation, even in the middle of a crowded room. Too often teachers and administrators work side by side in a common quest but fail to capitalize on one another's knowledge, skills, and experiences. The question becomes: What can school leaders do to ensure that their faculty members, including themselves, continue to grow and learn? It is the responsibility of school leaders to create a setting in which adults learning with and from one another becomes the norm.

DEFINING FACULTY COLLEGIALITY

Collaboration and collegiality sound alike and seem comparable, so it's easy to confuse the terms. In fact, collaboration and collegiality have quite different meanings. *Collaboration* refers to people working together to achieve a common goal; the result is better because of their joint efforts. *Collegiality* also describes a collaborative relationship, but there's more. When collegiality takes place, the product is better and the participants also learn with and from one another. Collaboration focuses only on the product; collegiality focuses on the product and what the participants gained from their collaboration.

A similar-sounding but quite different term is *congeniality*, which is important in every faculty lounge and every staff meeting. Faculty members should get along well and enjoy one another; if this is not the case, attaining collegiality is quite difficult. Indeed, as Robert Putnam notes in *Bowling Alone*, "Many studies have shown that social connections with co-workers are a strong predictor — some would say the strongest predictor — of job satisfaction. People with friends at work are happier at work." Congeniality, though, is not the same as collegiality; it is a base from which collegiality can evolve. School leaders need to be careful not to confuse the two and to avoid settling for congeniality. In this context, I often say that the job of the head of school is not to make teachers happy. To be sure, happy teachers are often better teachers, and I want happy teachers in my school. But to pursue happiness as a goal leads to a different set of behaviors and outcomes. Rather, the goal of school leaders is to create a setting in which everyone grows. When this takes place, happiness will follow.

The awareness of the importance of faculty collegiality stems from the work of Roland Barth. As a metaphor, he cites the instructions that are given to passengers about how to proceed when using an oxygen mask on an airplane. We are always told, he notes, that the adults should place the oxygen mask on their own faces before tending to a child or an elderly person. While this sequence is counter-intuitive to our desire to take care of those who need our help, the reality is that without giving ourselves oxygen first, we will not be able to help anyone else. We must take care of ourselves in order to be able to take care of others.

The parallels in education are quite clear. The adults (teachers and administrators) naturally focus on the children (our students). That's the way it should be; it's just not enough. We must focus on our students, but we must also focus on ourselves. The best teacher needs to be better, and the best administrator must also continue to improve. If faculty members are not growing and learning, they will become stagnant and students will lose. If faculty members are not working as colleagues, neither they nor their students will be well served. All teachers can learn from colleagues, and all students benefit when their teachers are part of a team. Likewise, if the head of school is not growing and learning, everyone is negatively affected. If collegiality is not the norm, a school cannot achieve its potential.

Barth identifies four distinct components of collegiality. Each is designed to increase student and faculty growth.

1. Teachers talking together about students
2. Teachers working together to develop curriculum
3. Teachers observing one another teach
4. Teachers teaching one another

Reflecting that administrators must be learners and colleagues, I add:

5. Teachers and administrators working together on educational issues

Teachers talking together about students. In most schools, teachers talk about their students, but, unfortunately, the dialogue is not always positive or productive. School leaders can help by asking questions and framing issues that are likely to stimulate discussion. These discussions are investigations in which all parties contribute and learn. In a collegial setting, faculty members talk about students' strengths and weaknesses, how and in what kinds of settings particular students learn best, and ways to work productively with their families. By structuring opportunities for teachers — this year's and last year's or teachers from this discipline and that discipline — to meet and talk about students, administrators can support this aspect of collegiality.

Teachers working together to develop curriculum. This also happens at many schools, especially those that are not wedded to state curriculum mandates, standardized tests, or both. Curriculum should be viewed as dynamic, always evolving to meet the ever-evolving needs of students and society. Everyone, including teachers from other disciplines or grades, becomes a resource. In a collegial setting, curriculum is always being evaluated and developed. School leaders can make this possible by providing times for faculty members to question assumptions about the curriculum.

Teachers observing one another teach. This occurs rarely, even in the best schools. Schedules are not conducive to peer observations, and, even more important, watching a colleague teach runs counter to the norm of isolation I described earlier. After all, giving and receiving feedback from peers can be a bit daunting. One way to address this anxiety is to "ask teachers to observe a peer with the goal of finding one thing they like and one idea they'll use," says Barry Roberts, principal of Warkworth Primary School in New Zealand. In a collegial setting, teachers know their colleagues' feedback can help them grow, and they understand that they can learn from observing other teachers.

Teachers teaching one another. This doesn't necessarily mean that a teacher stands in front of peers and imparts expertise. Although that can happen, the interaction that takes place at faculty and committee meetings offers richer opportunities for teachers to teach their colleagues. Sharing what did and didn't work yesterday, reviewing action research, presenting the content of a relevant article or book, and planning how to share the school's expertise with other educators — these all constitute teaching. The sharing of ideas that went into creating two books about our work with multiple intelligences at my school (*Celebrating Multiple Intelligences* and *Succeeding with Multiple Intelligences*) was a great way for teachers to teach their colleagues. In a collegial setting, teachers share their expertise with colleagues and further everyone's learning.

Teachers and administrators working together on educational issues. This can include myriad activities, from an administrator engaging in formal and informal classroom observations or meeting individually with teachers or groups of teachers to talk about goals, curriculum, or pedagogical issues to being an active participant on faculty committees that have an educational focus. Regardless of the activity, the administrator must be seen as a colleague. Teaching a class, laudable as that may be, only satisfies this need if the administrator's teaching responsibilities cause the faculty to view him or her as someone who understands and appreciates teaching, rather than as "an administrator who teaches." Particularly here, the head of school must be seen as a colleague. Writing in *Scientific American Mind*, Reicher, Platow, and Haslam note that "To gain credibility among followers, leaders must try to position themselves among the group rather than above it." Indeed, the need to be part of the group is heightened by the impact of technology on communication and on employees' expectations. In *The World Is Flat*, Thomas Friedman says, "Everywhere you turn, hierarchies are being challenged from below or transforming themselves from top-down structures into more horizontal and collaborative ones."

There are reasons why it's so difficult for a head of school to work collegially with teachers and to be engaged in the educational process. After all, the primary focus of teachers is education, whereas there are many noneducational issues that land with a thud on the school leader's desk. Investigating curriculum can seem like a frill when the success of the annual giving campaign will determine whether the operating budget is in jeopardy. Yet what I said at the beginning of this chapter remains true: Collegiality is the most important factor in determining the quality of a school. School leaders must not only work diligently to support collegiality among others; they must also be active participants in the collegial process.

FACULTY COMMITTEES

Faculty committees should be a school's R&D department, a place where academic research and development take place. While some committees are endemic to schools — a Social Welfare Committee and a Student Behavior Committee seem to be present everywhere — the true purpose of committees should be to help teachers work as colleagues in gaining knowledge. The following questions are ripe for committee investigation: Do our male and female students learn differently? Should we be offering AP courses? How can we incorporate altruism into our curriculum? What skills and knowledge should our graduates possess? How should our curriculum address the differences between success in school and success in life?

Questions like these offer opportunities for teachers to step back and take a broader view of the school than the one usually seen from the front of their mathematics, physical education, or third-grade classrooms. In every organization, it is necessary for leaders to help employees take the long view, and it is especially important for school leaders to help teachers see how their committee efforts make a difference. When teachers serve as leaders of a faculty committee, they also develop their leadership skills.

FACULTY BOOK GROUPS

An easy (and fun) way to encourage collegiality is by forming a faculty book group. I've done this for years and find it beneficial in many ways. Most im–

portant, the format supports collegiality very well. Teachers and administrators are learning with and from one another, and teachers are teaching one another; often, the dialogue evolves so that teachers are discussing students. Beyond the collegiality, this is also a powerful tool in raising or addressing educational issues. Books can be chosen that tie in with a school issue or curriculum focus.

Recently, for example, our faculty read *Mindset* by Carol Dweck. She distinguishes between the "fixed" and "growth" mindsets about intelligence, as discussed earlier in this book, and believes that how we define intelligence is a major factor in determining how smart we become. As you can imagine, this elicited spirited and productive discussions. Some of the other books we've read include *Frames of Mind, Emotional Intelligence, Boys and Girls Learn Differently! A Guide for Teachers and Parents, A Mind at a Time, The No. 1 Ladies' Detective Agency, A Whole New Mind,* and *"Why Are All the Black Kids Sitting Together in the Cafeteria?" And Other Conversations about Race.* I'm about to convene a group to read Daniel Goleman's *Social Intelligence.* Occasionally, I select the book, and sometimes faculty members choose. The group often meets before or after the school day, and we always have a group that meets over the summer.

Book groups vary in many ways, including what is read and when to meet, but I believe that there are a few constants that should be part of every group. First, participation should be voluntary. That may be hard for school heads to accept, but my experience is that making attendance optional works better. Only a minority of the faculty is likely to join, but because those who are attending choose to participate, the dialogue is far more likely to be open and positive. (The best advertisement for a future book group is the enthusiasm displayed by members of the current group.) Second, facilitation of the discussion should be shared. I typically begin with questions in the first session and then stand back so others can take responsibility. Finally, regardless of when the group meets, what is discussed, or who is present, providing food is always good. Paying for pastries or pizza sets a nice tone.

ADMINISTRATORS GROWING AND LEARNING

The involvement of school leadership is essential to faculty collegiality as well as to teacher growth and development. If students are to grow and learn, their teachers must grow and learn; if teachers are to grow and learn, their administrators must grow and learn as well. School leaders must be learners. We must invest in ourselves, too.

School leaders must be more than just learners; they must be *visible* learners. Everyone needs to know that the head of school continues to learn. We can show this to our faculty by being a partner in discovering how children learn and how to teach and by being part of the discussion about ways to measure student progress or involve parents. We can show our parent body that we're learning by sharing how we're involved and what we've learned. In my weekly letter, I often share what I've read with parents and talk about the implications for education (or life!).

Another way to be a visible learner is to make it clear that you do not have all the answers. Roland Barth talks about "the myth of presumed competence": People who run schools are expected to have all the answers all the time. And indeed, parents and teachers expect a knowledgeable leader. But that's not the same as someone who thinks he or she knows it all. It may be difficult to admit that you don't know the answer or that you'd do something differently next time, but it's important to do so. This is part of the Make New Mistakes philosophy noted in Chapter 1. Sharing that philosophy with staff members and parents helps set the expectation that everyone is expected to learn — and that learning can be messy.

THE IMPORTANCE OF LISTENING

One aspect of knowledgeable leadership is being open to new ideas and being receptive to feedback. As part of this, we must be good listeners. Listening well includes structuring in designated times when you *have* to listen and also ensuring that you listen to opinions you don't want to hear. That is neither easy nor pleasant, but it is necessary. Goleman talks about the danger that comes when "leaders expect to hear only messages that confirm their own sense of greatness." Granted, there are times when it seems that we only hear from the critics and carpers; I sometimes feel that way myself. But we can't let this deter us from reaching out and eliciting feedback and suggestions. No matter how often a head of school is standing and chatting in the hall or at a basketball game, it's necessary to offer formal feedback mechanisms to both staff and parents. School leaders need to create tools to help them listen.

I have found surveys to be effective in reaching out to parents. And depending on the age of students being served at a school, it may be wise to survey them, too. Surveying staff is also important. Again, perception is reality, so I need to know how my staff members view the school and me. The format that works best for me is to ask staff members to respond to questions that ask what I should "stop," "start," or "continue." What I'm really seeking are their thoughts on my weaknesses (what I should stop), things I should do differently (what I should start), and my strengths (what I should continue). This simple format of three one-word items seems to yield richer information than asking staff to directly comment on my strengths and weaknesses, even though the same points are being addressed. I always end all surveys with an open-ended item, such as "What other comments or questions do you have?" Responses can always be anonymous. (Surveys are discussed more fully in "Marketing and Admissions," Chapter 7.)

A few years ago, I participated in a "360-degree evaluation for growth." The term "360 degrees" captures the fact that feedback is generated from all sectors of the organization, not just from above. The term "growth" indicates that the data came directly to me, for use in my reflection and growth, rather than to a third party for the purposes of evaluation. Many organizations offer this service, and the format is generally the same. To start, I reflected on my strengths and weaknesses. Then online feedback on the same items was collected from several dozen people whom I nominated, people from all 360 degrees of the school, from trustees to staff to students' parents. A "coach" working for the company that conducted the survey then led me through an analysis of my profile, paying special attention to how my self-perceptions did and did not contrast with how others saw me.

The 360-degree data were also delineated by the respondents' roles so that, for example, I could see how I was viewed by staff members vs. students' parents vs. board members vs. how I saw myself. While all these data are helpful (and quite humbling), the differences in how I'm seen across the organization are particularly intriguing. I received a very good summary, but I also learned that I need to watch my competitive tendencies; sometimes this can come across as criticism of others. I also heard that at times my high energy and drive can be problematic; "Can you just slow the pace a little?" was one comment. There was no new or surprising information, which is good, but I heard some familiar themes to which I need to attend.

It's not unusual for perceptions to be tied to the organizational roles people occupy. Invariably, there are differences in how people in different organizational roles view our performance. For example, in *Legitimacy in the Academic Presidency*, Rita Bornstein comments on a common tension at schools: "Faculties accuse today's presidents of being too powerful; governing boards find them too weak." Hearing these different perceptions and expectations is the first step in balancing, if not resolving, them.

As you might imagine, this sort of listening can be very painful, but it's very necessary. Very few of us see ourselves as we are seen by others. The tools that are mentioned here — surveys and 360-degree evaluation — give us specific data about how we are perceived by others. That's the first step in enabling us to decide how to respond to their perceptions.

SUMMARY

A collegial environment benefits everyone. When collegiality is the norm, students, teachers, and administrators work together, learn together, and grow together. The culture becomes infused with learning, and the school becomes a setting in which success builds upon itself. Despite its simplicity, however, collegiality is not easily attained and maintained. School leaders must be willing to invest everyone's time and energy, beginning with their own, in the process of continued renewal through working and learning together.

CHAPTER 6

■

APPRECIATING DIVERSITY

A DIFFICULT LEGACY

"Schools like yours were created to exclude people like me," she said. There were about a dozen of us, independent school educators of various races, and we were meeting to talk about how to recruit students of color. The speaker, an African-American teacher from a nearby private school, threw this comment at all of us.

Her words were greeted with awkwardness and silence. I was both impressed that she had the courage to make the statement and saddened that there was some truth in what she said. After a few moments, a white administrator said, "I think you're generalizing. All of our schools weren't designed to be all-white havens..." He was cut off by another African-American teacher who responded, "No, not all, but most were." The room came alive with allegations, denials, and clarifications. Finally someone said, "This is all well and good, but our time is limited. Let's talk about what we can do now to increase the minority population at all of our schools. After all, we're meeting today because this is a goal that we share."

This story captures so many of the issues inherent in thinking about diversity in independent schools. (Note that I am not using the term *private schools*. The preferred term is *independent* because it more aptly describes how the schools function. Today's stances toward diversity are certainly captured in the differences between these two terms.) In the past, independent schools have not been seen as institutions that valued and pursued diversity. Sometimes this is because circumstances and context — tuition and location — have made it difficult for the schools to attract and support diversity. Sometimes, however, diversity has not been part of the mission of independent schools. Today, while attitudes have changed and independent schools are far more eager to pursue diversity, this legacy of exclusion may linger. Perception always lags behind reality, so leaders of independent schools need to make their schools' position on diversity very clear to both internal and external audiences. Then they need to make it clear again and, while doing so, make their personal positions on diversity clear as well. Perhaps more than with any other issue, parents, students, and staff look to see how a school's leaders think about and deal with issues of human diversity.

WHAT DO WE MEAN BY DIVERSITY?

Diversity can and should be defined in many different ways. Because skin color is so salient, we often default to talking about race when we think about diversity. Although geneticists have shown that the concept of race has no scientific basis, we still see race and thus we need to address race. Race is real whether or not it's real. But race is only one aspect of diversity. Socioeconomic status is another that is particularly relevant in independent schools.

But race and economics, important as they are, still do not encompass every facet of diversity within our schools. We are remiss if we don't consider individuals' physical abilities, scholastic abilities, learning style, gender, age, sexual orientation, ethnicity, culture, and religion. ("Considering" doesn't necessarily mean "embracing." A school for the gifted may want to accept only students who perform above a certain academic level. Likewise, a religious school may consciously choose to enroll a homogeneously religious student body.) Part of the role of the leader is to remind everyone in the school community that diversity is complex and multifaceted. This becomes even more important when the school community lacks diversity. Paul Geise, head of Pine Point School in Connecticut, shares his view: "The essential question is: How does the experience of an individual help inform and educate others toward a deeper and wiser perspective? At the end of the day, I believe the value of diversity lies more with the deeper understanding of the human experience and less with the racial, ethnic, demographic, socioeconomic, sexually oriented divisions we describe."

WHY DIVERSITY?

Indeed, the question of whether we want diversity within our schools can seem a bit moot these days: It must happen. Realistically, our schools must become more racially diverse in order to survive. In 2006, according to the U.S. Census Bureau, 43 percent of the school-age population (nursery school through grade 12) were students of color.[1] As Gene Batiste, NAIS vice president for leadership education and diversity, points out, "According to the *NAIS Opinion Leaders Survey*, about 65 percent of the population growth in the U.S. over the next 20 years will be minority, particularly from Hispanic/Latino and Asian immigrants."[2] It's clear that our country is going to become more and more racially diverse and that independent schools will need to reflect that evolution.

But demographic reality is only part of the issue. Our schools need to

---

[1] Compiled from U.S. Census Bureau "American FactFinder" tables.

[2] *NAIS Opinion Leaders Survey: Forecasting Independent Education to 2025*, online at *www.nais.org/files/ PDFs/OpinionLeadersSurveyJune05.pdf*.

become more diverse in order to prepare our students for the future. As we interact with others who are different from ourselves, whether this happens in person or online, diversity will become far more prevalent in every sector of life. Being able to live and work well with others who are of different races and backgrounds will become an essential skill. Writing in the November 2006 *Harvard Business Review*, Jeanne Brett, Kristin Behfar, and Mary C. Kern share what happens when diversity becomes a liability: "Multicultural teams often generate frustrating management dilemmas. Cultural differences can create substantial obstacles to effective teamwork — but these may be more subtle and difficult to recognize until damage has already been done." The changing face of our country and the increasing interconnectedness of the world mean that the ability to work in multicultural teams — indeed, teams that are more diverse in every respect — will be far more important tomorrow, and we need to prepare our students for this reality. A word I like to use in talking about preparing students for the future is *pragmatic*, a particularly relevant term when we are thinking about issues of diversity.

Al Adams, head of Lick-Wilmerding High School in California, speaks to the point when he says, "Another thing we have learned is that providing access to less-than-affluent families is not, in the end, about the school 'doing good.' It is, instead, about enriching the learning and living environment for all our students. Every student and his or her family bring a special set of gifts to contribute to the mosaic of the school community. Diversity, whether we mean economic, racial/ethnic, educational, or geographic, is, in the end, a vehicle for introducing students to experiences, understandings, ways of thinking, and ways of being that are different from their own." Similarly, Marcella Yedid, head of the Key School in Maryland, argues for diversity as an important aspect of preparing students: "Learning is maximized when students of differing abilities and backgrounds work together and develop an understanding of one another."

PROGRESSING TOWARD DIVERSITY

Diversity begins with enrolling and hiring people of color, but that is just the beginning because demographics are only one part of the solution. The question for school leaders is, "What can we do to increase and support diversity within all aspects of our school communities?"

Writing on the ISACS website (*www.isacs.org*), Lucinda Lee Katz and Bonnie L. Wishne cite the three phases of diversity presence in schools: awareness, commitment, and action. I insert another phase, "appreciation," between awareness and commitment. This appreciation occurs, ideally, from both a philosophical and pragmatic standpoint and creates momentum to support the pursuit of diversity. Thus, the continuum becomes four phases: awareness, appreciation, commitment, and action. Just as with learning how to calculate mathematical equations or play the piano, the phases are developmental and sequential. That is, awareness comes before appreciation, and both occur prior to commitment, which comes before action.

Reality, of course, is much messier than this depiction: There are jumps and starts, advances and regressions, and overlaps. What's significant, though, is that a phase shouldn't be skipped or glossed over. School leaders must resist the temptation to plunge into the action phase — developing strategies — before there has been sufficient awareness, appreciation, and commitment. This can be frustrating because we want to begin implementing diversity strategies *yesterday*! What's important, however, is creating a climate in which the action will be both successful and ongoing, and that requires an investment of time and energy in the earlier phases. Without sufficient awareness and appreciation, gains will be illusory and short-lived. (The NAIS Assessment of Inclusivity and Multiculturalism may be an effective tool for determining a school's position on the diversity continuum. For more information, visit *www.nais.org*.)

Regardless of how sequentially and developmentally a school progresses through the phases and regardless of the degree of enthusiasm and support for diversity within the school community, there will be difficulties. That's true of any effort in every arena, of course, but it can be even harder with diversity issues because they are so personal. Even at the most committed school, it can be difficult to discuss diversity at more than a superficial level because of the history and emotional baggage we all carry.

Years ago, I surprised another head of school when I said that one indicator that her school's efforts toward diversity were succeeding would be an increase of tension within her school community. As diversity issues become more prominent, questions and doubts will naturally arise. In too many settings, including some of our schools, diversity has been, at best, under the radar screen; diverse families, however defined, felt lucky to be present in the school and were reluctant to make any waves. When heads visibly support diversity issues and efforts, this shows value and gives voice to everyone in the community; that's good. But it's inevitable — indeed, it's appropriate, I told her— that caring people trying to forge new and better solutions will disagree; that's also good. (She later told me that my prediction was correct.)

The tension that comes with progress on the diversity continuum is captured by Tom Farquhar, head of the Bullis School in Maryland: "In a study of moral development in high schools [*Embracing the Tension* by McHenry et al.], done in the 1990s by the Friends Council on Education, we learned that the schools in our sample that had the lowest reported racial diversity (as a percentage of student enrollment) gave themselves the highest marks for 'tolerance' and 'acceptance of differences.' Conversely, the schools with the greatest measures of racial diversity rated themselves low on 'tolerance' and 'acceptance of differences.' This was an unexpected result."

Farquhar continues: "Follow-up interviews at the various schools revealed that when a small group of students bring a difference into the school community, they are 'guests' within the cultural norms established by the majority. When the proportion increases to a substantial segment of the school community, norms are contested, conflicts arise, and moral growth for all students and teachers is accelerated as these conflicts are discussed, addressed, and, sometimes but not always, resolved. Many of our independent schools have not reached the tipping point at which students who bring racial, religious, or economic differences to the school community are present in sufficient numbers to graduate from 'guest' status, which suggests that a great deal of the diversity work lies ahead for our schools."

His counsel is wise, and school leaders need to be aware of this potential problem and share it with their leadership teams and school communities. All progress takes time and energy and extracts a cost, and the quest for diversity is no different; the information from Farquhar helps set the stage for understanding and tenacity.

THE HEAD'S ROLE IN DIVERSITY

The head of school has a key role in assuring everyone that diversity is valued. More than this, heads must continually show their personal commitment to diversity. (This is the case even if there is a staff member who serves as diversity coordinator.) School leaders would like to think that their motives will be seen as pure, but that is not realistic, and they should not be offended when they are doubted. For many minorities, however that is defined, being skeptical or even cynical is a survival skill.

Invariably something will happen that can be seen as adverse to an appreciation of diversity, from a tuition increase to a decision on accepting a particular student to an approach to a topic in a class discussion. Particularly when there has been some sort of incident, the head's role is to share appropriate information and remind everyone of the school's commitment to diversity. Says Cheryl Milton Roberts, chair of the New City School board of trustees' Diversity Committee: "If people don't know the story, they'll create a story." Effective communication is always important but becomes even more necessary because of the potentially charged nature of diversity issues. Heads need to be direct and clear in addressing issues with diversity implications: They need to be direct by communicating quickly and explaining or clarifying, and they need to be clear by reminding everyone that diversity is valued in the school.

A significant step is for the school to employ a diversity coordinator. This may or may not be a full-time position; what's important is having someone besides the head of school who eats, drinks, and breathes diversity. The diversity coordinator must look for the diversity angle in just about every plan or action. This doesn't mean that all decisions are based on diversity considerations; it does mean that the implications for diversity are always considered. Sometimes schools will have a faculty diversity committee in addition; they may also have a board diversity committee instead of or in addition to that. What's the message if a school has faculty committees to deal with student behavior and academic achievement but not diversity?

Working with a school's full- or part-time diversity coordinator, a faculty diversity committee, or both, school heads need to ensure that diversity issues are an integral part of the formal and informal curriculum. Schools employ sectional administrators and department chairs, senior teachers, and assistant heads for curriculum, but with diversity, as with every other area, the ultimate responsibility rests with the head.

THE FORMAL AND INFORMAL CURRICULUM

A school's formal curriculum is what is stated, written, required, and taught. While the word *diversity* may or may not appear in the curriculum guide, the document says a great deal about how an institution values diversity. Is the settlement of this nation, for example, viewed simply as an advance based on "manifest destiny" and economic power, or are the needs and rights of indigenous people also considered? Is the Civil War taught as a series of battles and as a constitutional states' rights question, or is it viewed through the lens of many different protagonists? Surely there is much to be gained from looking at the issue of slavery from the perspective of a slave. What might be learned by studying the rationales of slave owners, despite how we may personally eschew their values?

The social studies examples are easy, but there are ways to inculcate diversity in other areas of the curriculum, too. Understanding the context that gave birth to the Arabic invention of zero or solving problems with an abacus to appreciate the sophistication of ancient China may take time away from mathematics but bring much to the students. Another example would be teaching an algorithm or calculation by comparing costs in different countries or with different kinds of currency. If the lesson is limited to simple calculations, though, an opportunity is lost. How is the lifestyle in the other countries different, and why is this the case?

This deeper analysis has implications not only for teachers but for administrators, too. Even when they're committed to diversity, there is often much that they do not know. This is captured in a story by Bonnie L. Wishne, head of the Ancona School in Illinois. In studying the civil rights movement, her teachers learned that Rosa Parks was not just a tired seamstress. According to Taylor Branch in *Parting the Waters*, she was a secretary at the local NAACP chapter and an activist. Wishne notes, "One Ancona teacher was furious when she encountered this version of the Rosa Parks story. In the name of multiculturalism, she had been teaching the other version from a respected children's book for years. Suddenly, she realized the truth was bigger and more complex than she had been teaching."

At my school, we look at many topics through a diversity lens. For example, our preschoolers create bar graphs based on the hair and skin colors of their classmates and teachers. Our fourth graders invite adults with physical disabilities to talk about the adjustments they've made and the discrimination they've felt. Examples abound at every grade and within every classroom. Diversity cannot be an add-on to the curriculum. In *Words Can Hurt You*, Barbara Thomson says, "To be effective, an anti-bias approach must be infused."

With older students, an easy and appropriate way to wade into diversity is to assign books written by authors who represent diversity. There is no doubt that all classes could read only books written by dead white guys and that the students would learn a lot, but what opportunities would be lost? There are many rich reading selections that provide the necessary content but also offer different perspectives. Choosing from among Margaret Atwood, Ralph Ellison, Langston Hughes, Toni Morrison, Amy Tan, and Oscar Wilde actually enhances the curriculum. The list of possibilities is almost endless, and it begins with an understanding of why it's important to read books by authors of different backgrounds and demographic groups. It is helpful for students to understand and appreciate this rationale and essential that they see their identity as well as others' identities in what they study. Doing this makes it clear that all groups have value and each individual is important.

The informal curriculum can be even more powerful and falls even more directly under the purview of the head of school. After all, the curriculum is often delegated to another administrator; the responsibility for the look and feel of the school resides with the head of school. The informal curriculum, an important piece of the school culture described in Chapter 3, encompasses much more than what is studied in class. In *The Art of School Leadership*, I wrote, "The informal curriculum consists of the routines, the practices, the policies, and the culture which guide our behavior; it is what we do. We may teach that the U.S. Constitution says that all men are created equal, but what do our actions say about how we value individuals who are gay? We may say that the Holocaust was a terrible event, but does our school accept and support a range of religious beliefs and is this respect evident when looking at events and holidays in the school calendar? We might say that we value human diversity, but what do the papers and work samples on the bulletin boards and walls say about which kinds of students and what behaviors are esteemed? These kinds of examples represent the informal curriculum."

The importance of the informal curriculum is supported by the comments of Al Adams: "It is one thing to open a school's doors to larger numbers of traditionally atypical independent school students; it is quite another to develop a culture that allows these students and their families to feel fully welcome and for these students to be able to bring their whole selves to school each day."

The informal curriculum also includes what is disseminated to internal and external audiences. It's not enough to feature faces of different skin tones in photos in the catalog; that's necessary but not sufficient. School leaders should intentionally push diversity by raising issues that will inform and, occasionally, disquiet. I make a point of explaining the holidays and celebrations of other faiths in my weekly parent e-letter, and I talk about how important it is to give students a diversity context to prepare them for the future. Important as these topics are, they're safe; no one could argue with their inclusion. But then I push the issue, challenging parents to think about their biases. A few years ago, for example, in one of my weekly letters, our diversity coordinator and I talked about how for historic and cultural reasons, it was even more important to our African-American families to be greeted in our halls by other parents. That elicited quite a bit of dialogue — quite a bit! — among and between both our minority and our majority families, and they were good exchanges.

More recently, our faculty diversity committee placed a huge piece of paper in the hall, and families were asked to use small adhesive circles to identify their family structure. The categories included mom and dad plus child/children, mom plus child/children, dad plus child/children, two moms plus child/children, two dads plus child/children, and other combinations. The presence of these categories raised everyone's awareness of the wide variety of structures in today's families and showed our support for all families.

The huge family structure chart hangs in our front hall, and while it was created to bring our current parents into the dialogue about family structure, it also serves a purpose with our prospective families. Its prominence means that most of them will notice it; we also point it out during our prospective parent tours. Many prospective parents embrace this inclusive look at families, but some are, we know, a bit put off by it. While we would like all families to want to enroll their child at our school, the reality is that not every family is comfortable with our philosophy on diversity and our related practices. If this is the case, it's far better for them to know this early in the process.

In addition to official comments at public meetings and in newsletters, heads can show they value diversity by initiating public conversations within and among the various groups at school. In describing this, Sheryl Reardon, my school's diversity coordinator, says, "Our evening parent events reflect our real commitment to diversity in its many forms. Families have the right to define themselves under our umbrella of diversity, which may be one of the most important and meaningful ways we show them that we respect them as they are and that diversity is more than just rhetoric at our school." We have regular meetings for parents of adopted children, for single parents, and for parents who are gay, lesbian, bisexual, or transgendered. As a way of supporting our economic diversity, we offer no-charge child care for these meetings (as we do for our open houses). One evening we offered a meeting for "nontraditional families" and let parents self-identify in choosing to join us. We've also had meetings for families of color (the term was chosen carefully so that it would include families with white parents and children of color).

DIVERSITY CAUTIONS

In responding to "What advice do you have for school leaders?" Cheryl Milton Roberts, chair of the board at New City School and past chair of the NCS Diversity Committee, has a caution: "Ensure that diversity at your school doesn't result in a stereotype. There is vast diversity among African Americans, Hispanics, Asians, and other groups. Ensure that this is clear. The reference point for an upper-middle-class black kid is not the same as for a lower-middle-class one. Puerto Ricans do not see any similarities between themselves and Mexicans, and people from China do not necessarily see themselves as being people of color." She notes, too, that diversity issues become even more complex when economic status and sexual orientation are considered. The bottom line is that we must be sure not to stereotype in our efforts to avoid stereotyping.

Some educators prefer to use the word *multiculturalism* as a way to better capture their encompassing approach. As Bonnie L. Wishne of the Ancona School says, "We have come to understand that true multiculturalism is a way of thinking, a way of approaching and questioning knowledge that transcends any particular body of content, because one thing we can be reasonably sure of is that the content that seems correct today will be outdated when our children are adults." Joe Marshall, head of the Orchard School in Indiana, defines the terms this way: "For us, diversity is identifying quantifiable differences, such as the percentage of students of color and percentage of same-sex families.

Multicultural education focuses more on the climate of the school; in essence, it's ensuring that our school possesses a culture in which all members, particularly those in historically marginalized groups, see themselves reflected and celebrated and know they are equal and vital members of the community."

SUMMARY

Whether a school uses the term *diversity* or *multiculturalism* is far less important than whether the school, led by the head, is a champion for diversity. At whatever level of the four phases of diversity (awareness, appreciation, commitment, action) a school finds itself, it is the head's job to move it forward. As with all important jobs, this may not be easy or fun. It is vital, though, to the future of our students and, indeed, to the world in which we all must learn to work and value others who are different from ourselves. This issue is too important to be left to chance, to assume that it will just happen because everyone is well-intentioned. School leaders need to take the lead in making their schools places where everyone thrives.

CHAPTER 7

■

MARKETING AND ADMISSIONS

MARKETING IS LIKE BREATHING

Marketing a school begins with listening to consumers and customers. It is a dialogue, an interplay among everyone involved in the purchase.

What? *Consumers, customers, purchase?* Isn't this a book for educators? Yes, it is, and I purposely used some terms that are often anathema to people who work in schools: *consumers, customers,* and *purchase.* We prefer to see ourselves as educators who operate above the fray. Our focus should be on creating the best school, curriculum, and lessons, and the rest will follow, we believe. If our school is good enough, prospective parents will find their way to our doors. Of course, there is a role for marketing and advertising, but those are tasks that are done by noneducators!

Perhaps one day long ago, marketing was handled totally by others. Maybe. This surely is no longer the case. Regardless of a school's legacy, reputation, and quality, marketing is a reality at every independent school, and administrators are integrally involved in it — or they should be. The demographics and perceptions of current and prospective parents are changing in many ways, and school leaders will need to become familiar with marketing principles and strategies. This includes but is not limited to heads of independent schools. As discussed in Chapter 9, public and private schools will become more alike in the future; while they will remain different in many ways, they will also share more and more similarities. All school leaders will need the ability to market their schools.

Society and technology have come together in a way that makes marketing increasingly important. In contrast to just a decade ago, there is now a wealth of information available on our schools through the Internet; paragraphs and photographs are just a few keystrokes away. Sometimes, they are *our* paragraphs and photographs, and sometimes they aren't. Consequently, the questions of what we present about our schools and how we present it have become much more complex and crucial. Parents are more discerning, too. The result is that marketing becomes a high priority, regardless of the strength of a school's enrollment or position in the community. Marketing allows us to enter and, ideally, shape the dialogue about our schools. Because marketing means working to better understand others' perceptions and needs, a focus on marketing can — indeed, should — result in a stronger educational program. Good marketing is good two-way communication.

I use the terms *consumer, customer,* and *purchase* to convey that when parents choose a school, they are making a rational economic decision and that we need to view them in this context. Parents might be uncomfortable admitting that their decision on where to send Carolyn or Carlos is guided, in part, by the capitalist's free-market "invisible hand" described by Adam Smith in *Wealth of Nations*, but it is the case. Regardless of a family's economic means, the decision to send a child to an independent school, and then to select school X over schools Y and Z, has an economic component. Certainly as a family's wealth increases, this component may be less important, but it is always a consideration.

Looking at our schools through this lens of economic choice illustrates that marketing is not only wise but necessary. An article I wrote for *Classroom Leadership* ("Consumers Versus Customers in School: What Are the Differences?") pointed out that educators too often focus only on the "consumers," the students, and ignore the needs of the "customers," the students' parents. That may be understandable given that most teachers and administrators choose education because they enjoy working with children, and it may make sense because teacher and administrative preparation programs give scant emphasis to students' parents (and the economics of schools). The fact remains, however, that failing to recognize that our students' parents are customers is a mistake.

Whether parents are writing checks for tuition or moving to a certain location in order to send their child to a particular school, they are making an economic decision; they are customers. A school head completing his first year said, "A big surprise for me was how much time I had to spend with our current families during the re-enrollment period. They had a lot of questions." It's clear that today's customers are more demanding than was the case a generation ago. Gene Batiste, NAIS vice president for leadership education and diversity, emphasizes this point: "As tuitions rise, parental expectations for measurable outcomes also grow. They want hard data about outcomes — college graduation rates, job satisfaction levels, and so forth." We need to take the time to educate and engage our students' parents. It is not enough for us to respond well when they want to be involved; school leaders should be reaching out and cultivating parents, informing and educating them. That's an important part of marketing.

Sometimes we may think of marketing as simply deciding what ads to use and where to place them, but marketing is different from advertising. In *Managing the Nonprofit Organization*, management guru Peter Drucker, quoting Philip Kotler, says, "The contrast between marketing and selling is whether you start with the customers, or consumers, or groups you want to serve well — that's marketing. If you start with a set of products you have and want to push them into any market you can find, that's selling." Marketing is, by definition, interactive. It embraces listening and eliciting. Advertising is raising the flag you like on a flagpole you choose. Marketing is gathering others' opinions about the flag; it's determining what qualities they want in a flag; it's educating them about the flag's meaning, design, and colors so they'll understand and appreciate the flag; it's determining the best location for the flagpole; it's generating enthusiasm for raising the flag. It may even be ascertaining whether or not others want a flag.

Schools need to advertise. Advertising is positioning the school — positioning the school's brand — in visible ways. Placing ads in newspapers and underwriting programming on National Public Radio seem to be common strategies. Announcing a Saturday open house with yard signs also falls within the realm of advertising. Finding ways to bring prospective parents into schools is always important. Liz Barnes, head of St. Paul's Episcopal Day School in Missouri, says that her school has used a direct mail piece from an advertising agency, a strategy that doubled the number of visitors to open house. Sandy Dean, retired head of the Philadelphia School, says that her students wore school T-shirts on trips to museums and other places. "People often stopped the teachers and complimented the students," she says. "I have received letters from strangers who were impressed not only with the students' behavior but with the knowledge they bring to the trips."

A different approach to the open house comes from Mary Worch, head of the Woods Academy in Maryland, who says, "Our open house is scheduled during a school day. In this way, prospective parents can see classes in action and get the feel of our school on a regular day. We use students and parents to give tours. The admissions director, assistant head, and I generally stay in the library to greet visitors and answer questions, and I personally meet with all new parents."

At my school, we've been offering monthly Story Time Saturdays, inviting neighbors with young children to come to our library for singing and read-aloud stories. This is a service we provide to our community, and it's also an effective way to advertise our school.

MARKETING IS ASKING — AND LISTENING

Unless they ask customers and then really listen, school leaders can only operate on assumptions they've made about others' needs. In the absence of information, they can only guess at others' motives: "They didn't send their child here because our program is too rigorous" or "Dad's business isn't doing well, so they couldn't re-enroll" or "We don't have enough diversity for them" or "We have too much diversity for them." Unless these leaders have asked and listened, these comments are merely hunches; they may or may not be true. Thinking we know how others feel without asking them or without gathering any data demonstrates no small amount of hubris. And yet, too often, school leaders base their strategies and programs on these kinds of suppositions.

When enrollment and donations are strong, it's easy to fall into the trap of thinking we know what students' parents want. The feeling that "They're standing in line to enroll, and annual giving has never been higher" may seem to provide shelter. Positive as these signs are, however, they do not eliminate the need to engage in formal marketing. Each year is new, and while past successes are helpful, they do not guarantee future achievements. Victories in schools are always ephemeral. Plus, each year's prospective parent body is a bit different from the previous year's. Societies and communities evolve, as do our schools' reputations. We always need to market; we always need to ask and listen.

THE SCHOOL HEAD'S ROLE IN MARKETING

Philip Kotler, quoted in Drucker's book, *Managing the Nonprofit Organization*, makes this role very clear: "Marketing doesn't get anywhere in an organization without the head of the organization getting interested in it, understanding it, and wishing to disseminate its logic and wisdom to the staff and people connected with the institution." That's the beginning. Then, once the head understands the significance of marketing, he or she must guide staff members in accepting it and ensure that the marketing messages are consistent.

Often, teachers view marketing as something schools shouldn't have to do and that they shouldn't have to consider. They often believe that admissions responsibilities fall only to the admissions office. A school head said to me recently with much frustration, "I can't get my faculty to see their role in marketing and enrollment." This is a missed opportunity. Faculty members need to appreciate that their involvement in marketing — from chatting with prospective parents who are touring the school to speaking at an open house or parent education program to attending students' sporting events or plays — means a great deal. Perhaps a way to approach this is by explaining the relationship of marketing to enrollment, and enrollment to financial health, and financial health to the resources that are available for students and faculty. I have found it beneficial to help my faculty analyze how other schools choose to present themselves and then think of the implications for our school.

A key aspect of the head's role in marketing, then, is helping the staff understand and embrace its importance. When this occurs, good things happen, as is illustrated in the following story from Billy Handmaker, head of the Crossroads College Preparatory School in Missouri:

> Many years ago, a prospective family was visiting the Missouri History Museum on a Sunday, and the family drove by our place on the way. The family had heard about us and had decided to drive into the parking lot and just look at the school. Our building manager happened to be working outside on that Sunday, and he saw the family drive up to the school and stop the car. He walked over, said hello, wiped off his hands, and asked if the family members would like to see the school. He ended up giving them a tour and discussing why he liked the school so much. They called us on Monday to talk to our admissions director and ended up enrolling both of their children. Dad eventually joined the board, and they were great supporters of the school. He told me many times that of all the things we did during admissions, the most memorable was when the building manager felt so strongly about his school that he was willing to stop what he was doing to give a tour on a Sunday afternoon.

Marketing should be viewed as everyone's job.

LISTENING TO PARENTS

What can heads of school do to learn what students' parents want and how their schools are seen? It starts with accessibility: School heads must be visible and receptive to hearing from others, including what they don't want to hear. Being open begins with listening without being defensive, often forcing oneself to wait before responding. This is much harder to do than to describe! Similarly, being visible sounds easier to do than is often the case. It's hard to find time to just be available, accessible, and around. But this, too, is an investment.

Whether he or she is greeting students and parents in the morning at the school's entrance or drop-off spot, roaming the halls at dismissal, or attending games, plays, and social events, the school leader needs to be routinely present. When this happens, it becomes easy for parents to ask questions or raise small points that are rife with big implications. It begins with relationships. In *The Guerrilla Marketing Handbook*, Jay Levinson and Seth Godin elaborate on this: "In order to sell a product or service, a company must establish a relationship with the customer. It must build trust and support. It must understand the customer's needs, and it must provide a product that delivers the promised benefits." When school heads are around and listening, they have opportunities to hear from parents who are happy, not just those who wish to carp. This also allows heads to ascertain the true nature of a parent's concern. As Joseph Michelli wisely observes in *The Starbucks Experience*, "You must be able to distinguish between people who want their concerns to be resolved and those who simply like to complain." Personally, while it is often hard for me to find the time to just "hang around" (because I have important things to do!), I almost always find it a worthwhile experience and am glad to have done so.

It's much easier to be visible with current parents than with prospective parents. Parents who are choosing schools aren't likely to be found at the game, talent show, prom, or carpool line. Typically, prospective parents visit a school only two or three times before making the decision about where to send their child. A good admissions director meets with them, asks questions, and listens, but even then, when possible, it's helpful for the head of school to be involved in some discussions with prospective parents. Much can be learned when heads hear parents' questions and the issues they raise.

USING SURVEYS

There are limitations to listening and talking — and to prodding and nodding. Realistically, there are only so many places a school head can be at once and only so many simultaneous discussions that can take place. There are also some families who won't be heard, due either to their lack of availability or to a reluctance to speak out. In any case, even though verbal comments are valid and rich, they are often casual comments. They can be tough to categorize and quantify and are affected by context and subject to interpretation. As a result, I advocate the regular use of parent surveys. Surveys give heads of school opportunities to hear directly from many parents, they present opinions in a more objective manner, and they help us sense shifts of opinion and emerging issues. Surveys can also be a very effective marketing tool.

Each May, for example, I send a Spring Parent Survey to all parents of current students. I am always pleased by the fact that most of the responses are positive and encouraging; I am also intrigued, though, by how ill-informed and off-base a few of the comments are, at least to my mind. Perception is reality, however, so I need to hear from everyone and ponder why the outliers responded the way they did. Most of all, I am aware of how the surveys give me insights into others' thinking.

A few years ago, I began to use electronic surveys. They yield a higher response rate (more than one-third of the families respond) and make data analysis easier. While issues and questions evolve, my survey always asks parents to agree or disagree with the following statements:

- My parent-teacher conferences were productive.
- The head of school, Tom, has been friendly and helpful.
- My child's individual needs have been met.

The survey also asks specific questions about our business and development offices, the amount of homework assigned to students, and our family support (extended day and summer camp) program. This book's appendix contains a sample Spring Parent Survey.

Surveys offer an opportunity to go beyond soliciting specific feedback to ask what parents want and what they value. I ask parents to identify the qualities that were essential for them in selecting our school. I make sure there are a few open-ended items, including one that simply says, "Questions? Other thoughts that you would like to share?" I end by reminding parents to let me know if they want a personal response from me.

Sometimes, I receive feedback on surveys that is quite critical. If I don't think the criticism has merit, this gives me an opportunity to clarify or explain. If, in fact, there is merit in the concern, this gives me an opportunity to apologize and begin to plan solutions. Sometimes, the criticism alerts me to a problem that wasn't on my radar screen. Regardless of whether I perceive the criticism to be valid, I want to hear it; hearing creates an opening for a conversation. As Michelli says, "The ability to act positively on any criticism is an essential leadership skill."

There are other logical opportunities to test the wind, too. In addition to the Spring Parent Survey, my weekly parent e-letters often invite feedback and reactions. After the fall parent-teacher conferences, for example, I ask, "How did your conference go? What adjectives would you use to describe it?" I raise similar questions after our Portfolio Night in May. Unlike the formal Spring Parent Survey, the response rate for these questions is never high, but that's okay. If parents do feel strongly, I will receive a reply. Most important, regardless of whether they respond to the surveys and questions, parents know I want to hear from them. (All my parent e-letters are available at *www.newcityschool.org*.)

PROSPECTIVE PARENT PERCEPTIONS

A customer is "someone who can say 'no,'" says Peter Drucker, and the school admissions process is all about customers' perceptions. Understanding perceptions is always an important part of leadership, and this is even more the case in the admissions process. Prospective parents, after all, have limited knowledge about the schools they are considering, so the possibility of misinformation and misperception is even greater. It's important for school leaders to learn how their school is viewed by prospective parents, both those who completed the process and applied for enrollment and those who elected to go to another school. Leaders need to know what prospective parents know and what prospective parents think they know.

For the past few years, my school has used an independent marketing firm to collect these data. Each summer, approximately 20 families receive a phone call from the marketing firm; they are asked a series of questions about their experience in the admissions process and their enrollment decision. Afterward, we receive a report that categorizes all responses (the respondents are not identified with their comments) and distinguishes between the perceptions of those who chose to attend our school and the perceptions of those who did not. Again, perception is reality, so it's very helpful for us to compare and contrast how we see ourselves with how others perceive us. The report also gives us a baseline against which we can measure changes in how we are perceived.

The heading at the beginning of this chapter, "Marketing Is Like Breathing," was chosen because school leaders are always marketing. Whenever we come across someone at a coffee shop, grocery store, or sporting event, we have our school's name tattooed on our foreheads. We may not like it, but whenever we encounter a present parent or student, a past parent or student, a prospective parent or student, or a potential donor, we are interacting as the head of school. It doesn't matter that this isn't how we see ourselves or even that this is not how we wish to be viewed. It is how others see us, and it's important for us to remember that.

IT BEGINS WITH ADMISSIONS

"Perception is reality" is a phrase I find myself using over and over again. Simply put, it means that people see the world differently and that they act on those differences. The following three stories speak to perceptions, and each has implications for admissions.

Chocolates on the pillows. The Williamsburg Inn in Williamsburg, Virginia, is a wonderful hotel. Travelers come from far and wide to stay there and be pampered. But as great as it is, I had an unhappy experience there a few years ago, thanks to the contrast with a nearby hotel, the Pirate's Inn.

My wife and I were meeting another couple in Williamsburg. As we were leaving home, running late as usual, I booked our stay at the Williamsburg Inn without paying attention to the cost of the room. Pampering does not come cheaply, however, and the price was steep. I didn't realize this until we checked in, and that still may have been okay. I like plush accommodations, chocolates on the pillows, and fresh fruit on the desk as much as the next person. But the couple we were meeting was staying three blocks away at the Pirate's Inn, and that became a problem.

You see, when we met them for dinner, we began to chat about our hotels. John told me what he was paying at the Pirate's Inn, and I was flabbergasted. It wasn't simply a bit less than I was paying. It wasn't even a lot less. It was a whole lot less. My room began to seem even more overpriced. My hotel offered a breakfast buffet on white tablecloths with soft piano music in the background; he had to go to a nearby doughnut shop to get coffee. "I'm paying what for tablecloths?" I wondered. And then, looking for perfection to offset the disparity in cost, I was bothered by little things — "Can you believe my coffee isn't hot?" — that I otherwise might have ignored. The cost of my room, in comparison to the cost of John's room, caused me to set such impossibly high standards for the Williamsburg Inn that I was bound to be disappointed. Had John not stayed at the nearby and incredibly less expensive Pirate's Inn, I wouldn't have felt so outraged. I mean, how could the coffee not be hot when the room cost this much?

I venture that not all parents at every independent school will feel this way, but some invariably will. Regardless of a school's quality, if it is charging significantly more than the parents anticipated, or more than they can reasonably afford, or more than they would like to afford, or more than what they perceive to be the alternatives, or even simply a lot of money, the parents are likely to have similar reactions. Rather than expecting limitless piping-hot coffee and chocolates on the pillows, they may expect their child to soar without a struggle or they may assume that the school will cater to all their needs. That sets the stage for disappointment. As tuitions continue to increase, this becomes even more common. A head of school is wise to ask: For which parents might this be an issue at my school? Or is it the case for all parents?

Cumulative dollars. Years ago, I heard author Tom Peters talking about his experience at a bookstore. As he was checking out, the clerk was rude and not very helpful, and Peters left, vowing never to return. "I would have spent $54 there, so the store lost a $54 sale," he said. "That clerk should have seen the $54 on my forehead and been more courteous."

Peters continued: "But as I was leaving, it dawned on me that I am a regular at this bookstore. I probably go there 10 times a year and average $41 in sales, so that's $410 per year." Peters paused for effect. "Moreover, I am likely to live here for at least another 10 years, so that's $4,100 in sales. This clerk just cost his store more than $4,000. He should have known that figure was on my forehead, but really, he should treat all his customers as if they have $4,000 plastered on their foreheads."

As I listened to Peters, I thought of my school. Our tuition then was more than $5,000, and many parents remain enrolled with us for nine years; that's $45,000 on each prospective parent's forehead. And what if they have two children? Today, our tuition is much higher, but the point remains the same (and is maybe even more relevant). Almost every prospective parent has a $100,000 figure on his or her forehead; current parents do as well. What does that mean for them? What does that mean for us?

Automobile dealerships. My wife and I own two cars, a Volvo and a Volkswagen.

They both run well and offer the same features. Despite the difference in price, her costly Volvo and my more economical Volkswagen seem very similar. That is not the case for the two dealerships' service departments, however.

The owners at the Volvo dealership know their clientele is high-end. When you take your car in for service, the room where you wait is a bit isolated, away from the noise and traffic, the chairs are comfortable, the floor is carpeted, and artwork adorns the walls. A courtesy phone is available. And when you pay your bill, the bookkeeper offers you a box of candy. Honest!

The Volkswagen dealership is another story. The cars are less expensive, and that's reflected in the setting. The waiting area is just that: an area and not a room. It's across from the desk where mechanics, service coordinators, and customers meet, so there's always a flow of traffic and busy conversation. The seats are made of hard plastic and the floor is tile. It's hard to concentrate because a shrill voice over the loudspeaker is continually asking someone in the parts department to pick up the phone.

This difference is also reflected in how the phones are answered at the two dealerships. A call to the Volvo dealership is answered quickly and transferred in a reasonable amount of time. I dread calling the Volkswagen dealership, on the other hand, because it takes forever for someone to answer the phone and, after that, I'm often put on interminable hold. A couple of times I've hung up and called again because I was tired of holding.

To be fair, it's possible that these differences aren't indicative of the relative cost of these two cars. I'm sure there are responsive Volkswagen dealerships and some unfriendly Volvo dealers, too. But this is my experience. While I like my Volkswagen, I am far less likely to buy another one, at least from this dealer. What messages do the differences in these two waiting rooms send to customers? What kind of clients are these two dealerships likely to attract and keep? The Volvo waiting area is more expensive, I'm sure, but it's an investment; it's a statement about the kind of customers that dealership seeks and wants to keep. What parallels exist within our schools?

BRANDING

Why should a family choose to enroll at your school? Let's assume there is an abundance of good schools in the vicinity, both public and independent. What sets your school apart? What features give your school a competitive edge? What is your school's brand?

In *The 22 Immutable Laws of Branding*, Al Ries and Laura Ries emphasize the importance of determining this: "Marketing is building a brand in the mind of the prospect. If you can build a powerful brand, you will have a powerful marketing program. If you can't, then all the advertising, fancy packaging, sales promotion, and public relations in the world won't help you achieve your objective." A school's brand should logically flow from its mission. It tells what sets the school apart. Schools are complicated organizations, to be sure, but it's important to find a simple way to capture a school's mission and uniqueness; that is the brand. "The power of a brand lies in its ability to influence purchasing behavior," say Ries and Ries, and as an example, they point out that Evian spring water is a successful product even though it costs more than milk or Coca-Cola.

In describing a successful branding program, Ries and Ries say that it "creates in the mind of the prospect the perception that there is no other product on the market quite like your product." Branding is creating an identity that is understood by everyone — insiders, outsiders, and prospective insiders. The reasons why a family should select your school must also be understood by current students' parents. They need to be able to articulate what sets "their school" apart. Some institutions have given their students' parents business cards with the school's name on the front and the school's distinctive characteristics on the back. These cards serve as reminders for current parents and can also be distributed to friends, colleagues, and prospective parents.

Board members can play a crucial role in branding because people expect them to have intimate knowledge of the school. The head and the board chair need to make sure this is the case and that board members know how to use this information.

Word-of-mouth recommendations are worth their weight in gold. A suggestion from Betsy Blankenship, the head of admissions at my school: "Look for ways to bring a broader range of constituents into your marketing efforts. For us, teachers, parents, board members, alumni, and neighbors have all played a role. More than 90 percent of all inquiries come because of word of mouth, so build on that."

The reasons for selecting your school are naturally the focus of conversation when prospective families visit the school. What other messages do parents receive? What is in your school's halls and on the walls? Sandy Dean, retired head of the Philadelphia School, says that visitors to that school saw "walls covered with art; every student is represented. This is marketing, not by design but as a natural extension of the learning." Likewise, what message does the signage give besides what the signage says?

Every school's website extols its fine academics, motivated students, and talented faculty; those are a given. What messages does your website give in its content and its appearance that set your school apart from the competition? Does your school's brand jump out from the site?

While schools spend a lot of energy attracting families and generating applications, they also need to spend energy in determining whether a child is appropriate for the school. This is an opportunity to market and reinforce the brand. How and on what basis a student is assessed, and how the results and the admissions decision are communicated to the parents, offer an opportunity for a school to make a statement about what it values. We need to remember that virtually everything we do, especially with families who are new to us, communicates something about our brand.

It can be argued that no staff member is more important than the head of admissions. (Indeed, that argument is often made by the heads of admissions!) The person in this position talks and meets with prospective families when they're investigating enrollment and plays a major role in the school's success. Obviously, this individual's skill in part determines who chooses to enroll. Is he or she friendly, knowledgeable, and organized? Each of these factors is important to the admissions process; conversely, if any one of these is lacking, fewer families will enroll.

ADMISSIONS STRATEGIES

The details of the admissions structure and process vary according to numerous factors. Certainly the size of a school is one important variable. In some schools, there is an admissions department with many people working side by side. Typically, in smaller schools, admissions is a one-person shop: There is simply a head of admissions. (And in some even smaller schools, the head of school is also the person who handles admissions.) Occasionally, parents of current students play a role in the admissions process. Prospective parents sometimes attribute a higher degree of verisimilitude to a current parent, and it can be helpful to tap into present parents' enthusiasm and experience. Parents who donate their time are volunteers, however — with all that this entails. As an alternative, using current parents to *supplement* the efforts of the admissions staff may be a good idea.

At some schools, prospective parents meet individually with the head of admissions. At other schools, parents are convened; for example, prospective parent coffees may take place at 10 a.m. on Tuesdays and Thursdays and at 1 p.m. on Wednesdays. (Within this structure, however, parents are typically given the option of requesting an individual tour.) Some schools begin by showing prospective parents a video about the school before meeting with anyone. Some tours whisk parents through the school, barely venturing into classrooms, while other schools allow — even encourage — prospective parents to linger in the building and spend time observing classes.

Regardless of size and type of school, there are some constants. As noted, the admissions tour guide must be friendly, knowledgeable, and organized. Technology is playing a bigger role in admissions these days, with periodic communications being e-mailed to families who are at various stages in the pipeline, but it all comes back to the individual who is the face of the process. For many families, this person *is* the school; he or she holds the hands of the family throughout the admissions process. That said — and without taking away from the role of admissions personnel — whenever possible, the head of school or another administrator or both should be introduced and should chat briefly with families. Many families feel it's important to spend a few minutes with the leadership of the school.

In most cases, prospective families tour the school with an admissions person. Often the touring group — ranging in size from two to eight — walks quietly into a classroom and observes for three or four minutes before moving on to another area of the school and perhaps another classroom. Before or after the classroom visit, parents are told what to expect or what was happening. This is fine, but it misses an opportunity. A very powerful strategy is to give prospective parents an opportunity to speak with current students. We do this routinely in my school (for both prospective parents and visiting educators), and teachers often create schedules that indicate which students will be the greeter at which times. This minimizes the disruption because the student who is greeting knows how and when to do this, and the responsibility rotates among class members.

I can appreciate the concern that this observance may interrupt the lesson, and it definitely interrupts the student who is doing the speaking. However, the impact this has on prospective parents — even when the greeter is not as eloquent as we might like — is always profound. Equally important, greeting strangers and explaining what's happening in the class is a good experience for students. I often join our prospective parent coffees after a tour, and when I do, I always ask, "What surprised you?" Our prospective parents are savvy consumers and have done their homework before they enter our doors for the first time. I want to know what was different from what they expected and in what ways we did not live up to how we market ourselves. The conversations are always interesting, and parents almost always comment on how impressed they were by our student greeters. Even when they are not our most polished speakers, they are always effective at generating enthusiasm for our school.

We currently offer a fall open house for prospective families on a Saturday morning. This is a productive time, with more than 100 families joining us. We track the attendance, and a good percentage of those who attend ultimately enroll. Occasionally, families come for years before enrolling; indeed, some begin attending when they are considering pregnancy! In order to engage this many people, we offer presentations by current students, alumni, and teachers. I offer a question-and-answer session, and current parents play the host and hostess role. We added this event fairly recently, and it has proven to be so successful that I wonder why it took us so long to offer it.

THE END OF THE BEGINNING

Too often, we view admissions as the sale. Indeed it is, but it's far more. A successful admission brings a new student and marks the start of a relationship — perhaps a lifelong relationship. What are the implications of a relationship that extends for 50-plus years versus one that ends next June?

Thinking about a commitment of several decades helps us recognize the importance of taking the time to invest in and build relationships. As part of that effort, we hold a welcoming party for our new families in April, after enrollment decisions are made but months before the start of the new school year. Current parents and staff meet with new parents to both applaud them on their choice and congratulate them on their acceptance. We also offer a new-parent dinner in late August, just before the start of school. We used to offer a meeting for our new parents at this time, but we recently began hosting a dinner instead. Here, too, some present parents join us. Our new parents seem to really enjoy the dinner, and it doesn't take away from our opportunity to welcome and explain. The cost of these events represents a good investment.

SUMMARY

Marketing and admissions work logically together. Indeed, sometimes it's hard to decide which heading best describes a particular activity (often because both fit). What marketing and admissions share is that they are both focused on building relationships. This requires planning, effort, and flexibility, but it begins and ends with listening.

And as important as both of these areas have been for independent schools, they will become even more crucial in the future. The combination of smaller demographic pools, increased competition, and higher tuition means that filling classroom seats will be a more challenging task for all of us. As noted, we will all become marketeres and everyone in the school will play a role in admissions.

CHAPTER 8

■

INSTITUTIONAL ADVANCEMENT

BUILDING BONDS

The focus on relationships is embedded in every chapter of this book. Whether the head of school is working with faculty members, students, students' parents, prospective parents, or trustees, relationships matter. Indeed, independent schools are often described as having a personal nature. Education is more than a transaction among parties, although it is that. The school is a community where students and their parents feel known and embraced. In good schools, children and their parents are each enrolled. I often hear parents say, "I feel a part of this school," "I'm learning here, too," and "When my child graduates, I am really going to miss this school."

The loyalty that is reflected in these kinds of comments develops because secretaries, teachers, custodians, and administrators are caring and welcoming. It happens because parent volunteers and board members reach out to parents by coaching teams and opening their homes for dinners and events. And it also happens because the head of school is seen as kind and caring. The head needs to be competent, knowledgeable, and skilled, but that is not sufficient. Relationships matter in every aspect of a head's role, and they especially matter in development.

Development, or fund raising, is based on relationships. That is not to ignore plans and strategies, and it is not to discount the role that donors' commitment to a cause and loyalty to an organization play in their decision. It is to say that people give because of their relationships. Their donations may be due to a relationship they have with a cause or a mission, or their gifts may stem from a relationship with an individual who represents an organization. Successful development requires creating an environment that causes people to want to give.

Donations, particularly significant ones, tend to be emotionally driven (and what is a significant gift for one donor may not be significant for another). The gift is more than a logical response to a need; it's an emotional response. Donors want to feel that their money made a difference and that children, probably their child, will benefit from their donation. They want to be valued as members of the community, and they want to feel that they did the right thing and can be proud.

Raising money for an independent school can be quite a challenge. After all, there are many worthy nonprofit organizations and causes pleading for donations, and some of them have a larger social impact than our schools do. It can be difficult to equate the importance of schools' missions with fighting hunger in Africa or Appalachia, curing cancer or AIDS, or providing relief for victims of natural disasters. But we can and must make the case for our schools, and with good reason. Without taking anything away from the many other worthy causes, gifts to independent schools are statements about hope for the future. Gifts to independent schools are both a desire for and an appreciation of excellence; they are an investment. A good development program makes that very clear and motivates donors to give more and in more ways than they had initially planned. Regardless of a school's niche, gifts stem from a donor's relationships with the school, its mission, and its individuals; indeed, when development is successful, gifts come from all of the above. Working with a host of others, the school leader must create a setting in which these relationships prosper.

INSTITUTIONAL ADVANCEMENT VS. DEVELOPMENT

In smaller schools, the head of school typically plays an integral and sometimes almost solitary role in planning, soliciting, and thanking. As the size of a school increases, the size of the development office grows as tasks increase in both scope and complexity. The head is still integrally involved in larger schools, but a distinction is often made between development and institutional advancement. These terms are closely related but different. "Development" typically refers to routine fund raising, including special events and annual giving. Institutional advancement is a broader term, encompassing development but also including marketing, advertising, and public relations; involvement with admissions and community outreach sometimes falls here, too. Alumni relations and periodicals/publications fall within both development and advancement (as well as marketing and, sometimes, admissions). Capital campaigns are certainly development, yet they may be lodged within institutional advancement.

The distinction between development and advancement can be murky. Because everyone is working toward the same ends — identifying, cultivating, and maintaining relationships — there will be a good deal of overlap. At times, the difference in responsibilities between the development or special events director and the director of institutional advancement may seem unclear. Likewise, there are occasions when the roles of development staff and the head of school will overlap. This duplication of responsibilities can be good or it can be counterproductive and inefficient. The head is responsible for determining who does what and keeping the roles clear and focused. Regardless of the size of the school or how it's organized, says Kathy Betz, former head of the Rossman School in Missouri, "Fund raising needs to be a fundamental reality of the school, a reality that is conveyed from the admissions process through graduation and into both the 'past parent' and alumni ranks."

FOCUSING AND SEGMENTING

It's neither sufficient nor wise to say that schools just need *more* and expect donors to write checks. The bumper sticker that says "It will be a great day when schools are well-funded and bake sales are held to raise money for bombers" has merit, but that's not the point. Our schools do need more (*all* schools need more), but that doesn't eliminate the need for planning and focusing. Indeed, precisely because the need is so great, we must be very thoughtful about both the purposes and strategies of our fund raising.

As with every other area of the school, the head and board must set priorities. The head, working closely with key board members (and perhaps a paid development staff), must focus and establish goals for the school's development efforts. This begins with ensuring that the school embraces the right attitude about development. Asking for sympathy from donors or appealing to their guilt is not effective. Kay Sprinkel Grace, author of *Beyond Fundraising*, says that nonprofits must "position themselves as organizations that meet needs, not as organizations that have needs." Answering the donor's question "Why should I give?" is the appropriate place to begin. "Why should I give?" always speaks to increasing an organization's ability to achieve its mission, but there are many valid responses schools might offer, such as those in the sidebar on the next page.

The differences that these responses, all worthy, illustrate in values and focus should not be overlooked. Just as good teachers differentiate among their students' needs and learning styles, good development programs differentiate among donors' capacities and interests. Helen Colson, author of *Philanthropy at Independent Schools*, has given this description of annual giving programs that thrive: "They segment prospects into many different groups. Each group receives separate fund-raising initiatives geared to gift potential, giving history, constituency, or the special purpose of the request."

WHY DO DONORS GIVE?

- To make up the gap between what the school charges and what it costs.
- To enable economically disadvantaged students to attend the school.
- To enable the school to provide a high-quality program.
- To enable the school to widen its high-quality programs.
- To create an endowment fund for the future.
- Because they want to feel a part of the school's mission.
- Because they want to be recognized as participants in the effort.

The operating budget typically includes annual giving, so the case can be made that everyone's first gift should go to the annual fund. At times, however, it may be wise to also segment donors (or perhaps donors at a certain giving level) by their interests. Offering donors the opportunity to designate their gifts may encourage more generous giving. What excites donors? Would a donor prefer to make a gift to fund a building renovation, or would he rather bring foreign language instruction to the school? Is the donor excited about supporting professional development for teachers, or does she want to see more students receive financial aid? Appealing to a donor's passion can be a win-win for everyone. Heads of school must be sure, however, that the menu of needs offered to donors is worthy and supports the school's mission.

An example of a donor giving to fund a passion is captured in the story a secondary school head told me about how his school's new artificial football turf is better than that of the local NFL team. "A donor walked in one day and said he'd like to buy new turf for us," he told me. "His son is on the football team. We were surprised by the offer because that wasn't one of the priorities in our capital campaign, but we talked about it and agreed that we needed to improve the field, so we were happy to accept the gift." The important point in this story is that the school leadership decided there was a need for new turf and that made the gift acceptable. A donor may be interested in funding an international chess competition, but if that doesn't fit with the school's mission and program, the funds should not be accepted. Declining a gift can create a difficult situation. Ideally the donor can be led to see that funding a solar automobile competition is just as exciting as sponsoring a chess tournament, but if not, the school should politely refuse the offer, hard as it may be to do so. Again, the head's job is to protect the school's mission and programs.

Ginger Imster, director of development for the City Academy in Missouri, captures this potential for conflict when she says, "So often projects come up that can be potentially exciting but also very distracting from the school's immediate needs. It's the head's job to be certain that all gifts are mission-driven. That being said, I think most heads also recognize that gifts need to be budget-driven, too. There can be exceptions, but they should be rare, and it's the head's role to keep everyone focused on the budget while at the same time being mindful of donor preferences and priorities."

Arguments can be made for and against segmenting donors by their interests, but there is much less dispute around donors being segmented by their giving potential. It only makes sense that the approach used when asking for a $1,000 donation should be different from that used when seeking $100, for example. Decisions about which approach to use at which dollar figure must be made at each school and should reflect the school's history and needs. At some schools, a $1,000 giving request warrants an individual meeting with the donor by the head of school and board leadership. At other schools, a personal meeting may occur at a much higher or lower giving level.

DEVELOPMENT CAN BE HARD ON RELATIONSHIPS

Tensions can arise. Recognizing that a gift of $10,000 is worth 10 times the value of a $1,000 gift, the head is also responsible for making it clear that *every* gift is valued. This can be difficult because while every gift is important and every donor receives a personal letter of thanks, that appreciation is sometimes acknowledged in different ways. Many schools hold donor appreciation parties to thank those who have given, and sometimes a gift must be above a certain level in order for donors to be invited. We do this at my school and find it an effective way to both thank and cultivate. It's important for donors to see others who give at a comparable level. Segmenting appreciation for donors by their giving level has its drawbacks, however, and does not come without a cost.

An appreciation party for higher-level donors may be a good tactic, but school heads are naive if they think that only those donors who are invited will be aware of the party. Even if the party is held off campus, word about the event will leak (and trying to offer a "secret party" is even worse). Some parents who aren't invited won't care and some who aren't invited will think the strategy is wise, but others will take offense at a party for "the select few." Some parents will also be unhappy that money is being spent to raise money "instead of educating our children."

In a way, this tension about development strategies is not surprising because an economic range among students' parents exists at virtually all schools. The size of the range will vary, but some parents will always have greater resources than others. That disparity is true throughout life and in every arena, but it can sometimes be more obvious in a school. After all, we may not live or work next to people who have far more or far less money than we do, but we can wind up sitting next to them at the open house, spelling bee, or football game. Fortunately, students often handle the disparity in dollars better than their parents do; students see the range of resources through the context of their experiences at the school and often think, "He has more money than I do, and so what?" (Students typically also have an easier time forging friendships with peers of other races and cultures than their parents do.)

Some adults without these kinds of experiences, however, can be very sensitive to donors being treated differently based on giving levels. Some may even assume that children of parents with ample means receive preferential treatment from teachers and administrators. After all, significant resources often result in privilege elsewhere in life, so why shouldn't it be that way at a school? The fact that the head of school is visible in fund raising may fuel this impression. Consequently, an important part of the head's role in building relationships is to make it clear that fund raising is important and that the school does need generous donors in order to provide an excellent education for every student. However, the head also needs to emphasize that all gifts are important and appreciated and that every child receives all the advantages of the school, regardless of whether his or her parents are donors or whether they donate significantly.

This can be difficult because often it is the parents with the greatest resources who are most able to become involved with the school. When parents are selected to join the board of trustees, wealth is certainly a consideration, along with wisdom and willingness to work. This means that heads can find themselves working most closely with those who are the most generous donors. The leadership visibility of big donors can exacerbate the tension felt by those who cannot give as much, regardless of their loyalty and personal generosity.

Again, part of the head's role is to assuage these tensions. It's important to take them into consideration when school events and development strategies are planned. Are there free or inexpensive events to which all families are invited? Are all donors' names listed in the annual report, and is everyone thanked with sincerity? Are there opportunities for parents to get involved in the school and with the parents' organization and board of trustees, regardless of their ability to donate? Finally, and far from least important, with whom does the head chat casually in the halls and at games? Is the head an equal-opportunity chatter, or is more time spent with those whose names are at the top of the donor list? Believe me, people notice the little things, and in building relationships, the little things are often the big things.

TODAY'S PARENTS

While answering the "Why should I give?" question has always been essential, it is even more important to answer it well when we are working with today's parents. First, many of them are new to independent education and are often surprised to see that they are asked to donate beyond what they pay for tuition. This will become even more of a factor in the future as independent school enrollments diversify and schools enroll more students who receive financial aid, more students of color, and more students who are children of immigrants, all populations with less independent school experience. (See Chapter 9 for demographic data on the future.)

In *Philanthropy at Independent Schools*, Helen Colson says, "Today's parents think more like consumers. They are making an investment, so they are interested in the nature and quality of the return." The consumer mindset may be caused by the fact that some, perhaps many, parents are Generation Xers, born between 1965 and 1980. The legacy of the Vietnam War and Watergate helped frame an attitude of doubt among this generation. In describing the attributes of Gen-X employees in *Beyond Generation X*, Claire Raines says that "they are not intimidated by authority" and that their view of authority is "unimpressed." Similarly, in *When Generations Collide*, Lynne Lancaster and David Skillman say that "Xers have been marked by skepticism." It may seem ludicrous to a parent who is both new to independent education and a Generation Xer to pay tuition and then be solicited for a gift.

The response to these questions and attitudes lies in parent education. Parents need to understand why tuition doesn't cover the cost of education, that their gifts are necessary to improve the quality of education, and that every gift is important, regardless of the amount. School leaders need to make parent education a priority.

THE HEAD'S ROLE IN DEVELOPMENT

Invariably, heads of school spend more time on development than they planned (and often more than they would prefer). Development and marketing are integral parts of every head's job, and this seems to be more and more the case each year. As the competition for dollars and students increases, heads of school wind up spending more time on institutional advancement. Cultivating donors and educating parents are both important, and each can take a considerable amount of the head's day (and evening). "A head must establish connections with all constituents on a regular basis as a part of basic, day-to-day leadership.

Those friendships and connections are the things that promote believability when it's time to ask for larger or even smaller gifts," says Kathy Betz.

How much time do heads spend on these activities? "Committing 20 percent of their time to fund raising is common for school heads," Colson says. "However, some devote 40 to 50 percent, particularly during a capital campaign." My personal experiences, as well as comments I hear from other heads, suggest that Colson's higher estimate is accurate. That seems like a lot of time — it is a lot of time! — but an elucidation of the head's responsibilities shows why this is the case. Colson notes that there are many components to the head's development role. The head is the chief communicator of the school's vision, the leader of the development team, the major gift cultivator, the solicitor of leadership gifts, and the supervisor of the development office. And not to be overlooked, she says: "It is the head's particular responsibility to convey deep gratitude to the top volunteers who give generously of their talent and time."

Sometimes faculty members complain when I am not in their classrooms as much as they (and I) would like. Occasionally, someone will remark about how much better it was years ago, when I popped into his room on a regular basis. I share these sentiments. As noted in my thoughts on collegiality (Chapter 5), it's important for the head to be a working member of the faculty. Good things always occur when I'm participating on a faculty committee or observing a lesson in a classroom. As this chapter illustrates all too vividly, however, it's harder and harder to find the time to do this. Many of the development tasks simply cannot be delegated.

Faculty education becomes important. Heads of school need to find ways to share their professional challenges and explain how they're spending their time. It's helpful for teachers to understand why they may not see the head of school as much as they would like. (I can't complete this section without noting that I'm always flattered when teachers complain that they wish they saw more of me or had greater access. That's a good sign!)

Heads need partners in their development efforts. While the head of school should participate in important personal solicitations, a peer of the potential donor (a board member or other volunteer) should accompany the head and do the official asking. The head and volunteer work as a team: They set the tone, update the donor on what's happening at the school, and make the case about why the gift is needed. But the volunteer is the one who pops the question: "I'd like you to consider making a donation of $XYZ to help us succeed..." or "I'd like you to match me in giving $XYZ to...." Although it may seem to be a small distinction, this method reduces the appearance of a link between an individual's gift and preferential treatment of students. The approach also reinforces the institutional, rather than personal, nature of the ask. (Plus, having a partner makes it easier to catch your breath, think, and compare notes after the visit.)

SPEAKING THE VISION

Once the reasons for giving have been determined, an important aspect of the head's job is to articulate the vision. "Vision leaks. It needs to be communicated clearly, creatively, and continually," says John Maxwell in *The 360 Degree Leader*. As noted in Chapter 1, the head of school never misses an opportunity to express the school's vision and mission, ideally in a few succinct words. Similarly, without suggesting that there are dire problems, the head needs to clearly present the school's needs to donors. Doing this repeatedly can be a challenge, because like all important messages, it must be delivered again and again. And again.

Once, at an open house when we were educating our students' parents about the importance of financial aid, the chair of our development committee came to the stage and said, "I have a dollar bill" — he held it up — "for the person who can correctly tell me what percentage of students here receive financial assistance." Hands were raised here and there, and numbers shouted. Finally, from the side, one wise parent said, "Is it one hundred percent?"

"Yes," replied the chair of development, as he walked over and gave away his dollar. "You see, tuition doesn't cover the cost of our expenses. There's a

$1,500 gap for each child, so every student here, every one of your children, receives financial aid. That's why annual giving is so important to us." Donors need to know the school's needs, how the school can improve, and how their gifts will enable the school to do better. However, it's important that gifts be requested from a position of strength, to be used to improve; it's easier to get gifts to achieve success than to avoid failure.

CULTIVATION

Simply put, cultivation is building the relationship between the donor and the institution. Cultivation is bringing the donor into progressively tighter inner circles, engaging the donor in a conversation, and involving the donor in solutions. Many people — certainly board members and other administrators — can and should be part of the cultivation process, but this often falls to the head of school. By virtue of his or her position, there are many times when the head needs to be at the table.

Another good strategy for cultivation is to include non-trustee parents on trustee committees. This broadens the conversation (and can also serve as an opportunity to determine who might be appropriate to join the board in the future). Periodically, I have "Coffee with Tom" sessions for anyone who wants to come and chat. Often a comment in my weekly parent e-letter will elicit many responses (such as the time I asked parents to share their definitions of success). Most important, though, I receive a constant stream of e-mails from our parents. Some complain and some praise; many are reflections or questions; all are opportunities to get to know the parent a bit better and a chance for cultivation.

In a perfect world, every individual would be cultivated. But the world isn't perfect, and given the limitations of time and personnel (and inner circles), we focus our efforts on those who can help us advance our schools. Advancing our schools goes beyond donors, of course, although it definitely includes donors. Skilled parents and friends can help us, even if they aren't in a position to write a large check. Their donation may be in the form of work or wisdom.

Cultivating them is an important part of the head's job, too.

Cultivation results in a solicitation, and the head cannot and should not be the only solicitor. As mentioned earlier, peers should be involved. Not only is this a more effective technique, but involving others in "the ask" is the best way to create a context for them to make gifts. The individual doing the asking should have already committed to a gift that is equal to or greater than the gift being solicited. Just as the best way to learn something is to teach it, the best way to get a donor to embrace a cause is to have the donor solicit for it. Indeed, having donors solicit is a wonderful way to cultivate them.

APPRECIATING APPRECIATION

The cardinal sin of development is to take donors for granted. This is true whether the donations are large or small and whether the donors give dollars or time, whether they give expertise or spread the word among friends and neighbors, whether they are first-time donors or have been giving for years. In fact, it's true if the donors simply entrust the school with their children. Donors must be appreciated and recognized. How that happens will vary by institution and individual, but it must happen.

Thanks should be prompt and personalized as much as possible. The head of school should sign all thank-you letters, sometimes with the additional signature of the chair of a particular effort or the chair of the board. Technology makes it much easier to send a raft of personalized letters, with the recipient's first name in the greeting and a signature in ink of a different color, to many, many people. Effective as that is, it only makes the personal handwritten note, even if sometimes a bit illegible, more important. Scrawling a few words of appreciation across the bottom of a computer-generated "personalized" letter is good; taking the time to send a separate, handwritten note is even better.

SUMMARY

Donors give to causes, but the causes usually have faces. The faces may belong to those who will benefit from the generosity (students or staff members) or to the donor's colleagues. In any case, the donor gives (or gives more) because of a personal connection. The head of school plays an integral role in establishing and cultivating these connections and relationships. The head's presence is a crucial factor in public sessions and private meetings, and the head's judgment is important in determining strategies and expressing gratitude. There is never enough time to do all that is necessary, but heads of school must find the time to advance their institutional advancement programs.

■

CHAPTER 9

THE EVOLUTION OF LEADERSHIP

FOUR CERTAINTIES

Looking around the corner is always difficult. Despite our abundance of technological tools and theoretical models, we really cannot know what the future will hold. Who could have predicted the Internet 15 years ago, much less envisioned how it would affect communication and commerce? When President Eisenhower proposed the interstate highway system 50 years ago, who could have known the impact it would have in creating suburbs and depleting urban areas? And 75 years ago, with our country in the throes of a depression, who could have imagined today's lifestyles or geopolitical interests and conflicts? Predicting the future is always risky.

That said, there are four areas in which the direction for our future is relatively clear: technological advances, economic competition, emotional intelligence, and human diversity. In each of these areas, we can speculate with some degree of confidence, so much so that I refer to them as "certainties," although perhaps, as you will read, nothing is truly certain, including death.

One certainty is that tomorrow's world will be faster-paced and even more extraordinarily complex. Since the advent of the Industrial Age, access to new technology has always increased the rate of change for each succeeding generation, but it has never moved this quickly. In *Fantastic Voyage*, Ray Kurzweil and Terry Grossman note that the speed of progress in the 21st century will be "1,000 times greater than what we witnessed in the 20th century, which itself was no slouch for change." Technological solutions will be applied to virtually every problem and human condition, even raising the *un*certainty of death. Kurzweil and Grossman cite Aubrey de Gray, a researcher on aging, in saying, "We will successfully stop aging in mice, who share 99% of our genetic code, within 10 years, and … human therapies to halt and reverse aging will follow five to 10 years after that." (To be fair, I would be remiss if I did not also acknowledge that technological gains and promises do not come without a cost. Global warming is perhaps the most obvious example of unintended consequences, and there are others.)

A second certainty, noted in Thomas Friedman's *The World Is Flat*, is that global economic competition will increase; in fact, this has already happened. As noted, technology is a major factor in this because it removes considerations of distance and political boundaries from most work. (There are no borders on the Internet.) As Friedman notes, "No matter what your profession — doctor, lawyer, architect, accountant — if you are an American, you'd better be good at the touchy-feely service stuff, because anything that can be digitized can be outsourced to the smartest or cheapest producer or both."

Nowhere is this clearer than in the economic role that China's size will cause it to play around the globe. On the first page of *China, Inc.*, Ted Fishman puts this in perspective: "China has between 120 and 160 cities with a population of one million or more (America, by contrast, has nine, while Eastern and Western Europe combined have 36)." In explaining how these numbers will affect the rest of the world, he says, "China is the world's workshop because it sits in a relatively stable part of the globe and offers the world's manufacturers a reliable, docile, and capable industrial workforce, groomed by government-enforced discipline." As Fishman says, "... companies can move nearly any kind of work to China and find huge savings." Production in China is not without drawbacks, as we've seen in pet food, toothpaste, and lead paint, but its economic incentives are powerful.

Visions of the future are both mind-boggling and a bit frightening — mind-boggling because it seems that virtually anything is possible and frightening because it seems that virtually anything is possible. And yet despite (or perhaps because of) the power of technology, interconnectivity, and speed of change, the third certainty is that our ability to use our minds and work effectively with others will become even more important.

Successfully competing on "the flat Earth" that Friedman describes, one in which our competitors can be next door or a continent away, will require strong sets of interpersonal and intrapersonal skills. Our students must be trained to be leaders and followers and collaborators. The ability to work as a team member and play a variety of roles will be even more important than it is today. The power derived from these interactions is captured in *Social Intelligence* when Daniel Goleman says, "We create one another." Technology will increase the quantities and kinds of people we interact with, making it easier to establish relationships. In all likelihood, however, reliance on technology will make it more difficult to develop those relationships.

In *A Whole New Mind*, Daniel Pink says that jobs are vulnerable if they are routine, if they can be done by a computer, or if they can be performed more cheaply overseas. Making a case for creative, right-brained thinking, he says that what will be needed in the future will be thinking that is "high concept" and "high touch." "High concept," according to Pink, is "the capacity to detect patterns and opportunities, to create artistic and emotional beauty, to craft a satisfying narrative, and to combine seemingly unrelated ideas into something new." He defines "high touch" as "the ability to empathize with others, to understand the subtleties of human interaction, to find joy in oneself and to elicit it in others, and to stretch beyond the quotidian in pursuit of meaning and purpose." This description is very similar to the desired skills noted by Daniel Goleman in *Emotional Intelligence*: "Much evidence testifies that people who are emotionally adept — who know and manage their own feelings well, and who read and deal effectively with other people's feelings — are at an advantage in any domain of life, whether romance and intimate relationships or picking up the rules that govern success in organizational politics."

International cooperation and competition will result in work relationships

IN THE YEAR 2050...

- Nearly 67 million people of Hispanic origin (who may be of any race) will be added to the nation's population between 2000 and 2050. Their numbers are projected to grow from 35.6 million to 102.6 million, an increase of 188 percent. Their share of the nation's population would nearly double, from 12.6 percent to 24.4 percent.

- The Asian population is projected to grow 213 percent, from 10.7 million to 33.4 million. Their share of the nation's population would double, from 3.8 percent to 8 percent.

- The black population is projected to rise from 35.8 million to 61.4 million in 2050, an increase of about 26 million or 71 percent. That would raise their share of the country's population from 12.7 percent to 14.6 percent.

- The country's population is also expected to become older. Childbearing rates are expected to remain low while baby boomers — people born between 1946 and 1964 — begin to turn 65 in 2011. By 2050, more than 20 percent of the U.S. population will be 65 or over.

- The female population is projected to continue to outnumber the male population, going from a numerical difference of 5.3 million in 2000 (143.7 million females and 138.4 million males) to 6.9 million (213.4 million females and 206.5 million males) by mid-century.

Source: U.S. Census Bureau, "U.S. Interim Projections by Age, Sex, Race, and Hispanic Origin," March 2004; online at *www.census.gov/ipc/www/usinterimproj/natprojtab01b.pdf* and *www.census.gov/ipc/www/usinterimproj/natprojtab02a.pdf*.

being forged around the world, both face to face and online. In addition, the United States will be a far more diverse nation (see sidebar on the previous page). Consequently, the fourth certainty is that we will all need to work well with those who are different from us.

The increased diversity may not, alone, be cause for optimism. In the July 6, 2007, *New York Times*, columnist David Brooks writes, "It could be that [the dream of integration itself] was like the dream of early communism — a nice dream, but not fit for the way people really are." Humans are conditioned to distinguish between "us" and "them," he says, and while "People say they want to live in diverse integrated communities, what they really want to do is live in [communities] filled with people like themselves."

He continues, pessimistically: "[M]aybe integration is not in the cards" and "Maybe the health of a society is not measured by how integrated each institution within it is, but by how freely people can move between institutions." Brooks concludes, "This isn't the integrated world many of us hoped for. But maybe it's the only one available."

The good news is that Brooks may be incorrect and that increasing diversity may lead to greater understanding. As Gene Batiste, vice president of leadership education and diversity at NAIS, notes, "In looking at the global community in which you will be living, it is imperative that we focus on the fact that there is no substitute — no matter how much we read about different cultures — for living on a daily basis with people who are different." The increasing presence of human diversity alone does not equate to acceptance, understanding, or appreciation. "At times, folks from these varied backgrounds coexist and thrive in harmony, at other times with discord," Batiste says. This means that school leaders have an obligation to ensure that schools seek not only greater demographic diversity but also greater understanding and appreciation.

THE FUTURE OF SCHOOLS

School leaders will need to grapple with the fundamental certainties of change, both internally and externally. The internal struggle will focus on curriculum, pedagogy, and preparation of students, as it always has. The task of preparing for tomorrow is different from the task of preparing for today, but this is familiar territory. Good school leaders have always focused on what their students need in order to succeed in the real world. Externally, however, the conditions in which schools exist will change considerably. School leaders will need to respond not just to demographic shifts but also to the changes in public and private education and assessment in this country.

They will need to offer enough technology to enable students to be comfortable with it and know how it can help them solve problems. They must resist the temptation, however, to view technology as more than a tool, despite how exciting and alluring the hardware and software can be. The difficulty in maintaining this balance is exacerbated as technology becomes more pervasive and students' parents become more dependent upon it. ("Why can't my 10-year-old bring her cell phone to school?" a father recently asked me.)

School leaders will also need to focus on teaching students how to identify and solve problems. As problems become more complex, correctly analyzing them — "What is the question, what information do I need, and who can help me solve it?" — becomes part of the solution. Another way to look at this is that a part of preparing students is helping them develop their distributed intelligence, which I described in Chapter 2 as the degree to which one can capitalize on resources in the environment to solve a problem. This might be knowing how to use available technology or understanding how the Dewey Decimal System works, or it might be appreciating the various talents and interests in a peer group and knowing who can help solve the problem. Rarely are important problems solved by one person, so teaching students how to be part of a problem-solving team is important.

Walking the fine line between traditional learning on one hand and creative, right-brained thinking on the other is not easy. Our students must possess the necessary basic skills, but that is just the beginning. We cannot stop with the mastery of facts and acquisition of knowledge any more than we can begin with creativity and higher-level problem-solving; both are essential. In

Educational Leadership a few years ago, Elliot Eisner wrote, "The primary aim of education is not to enable students to do well in school, but to help them do well in the lives they lead outside of school."

As part of the focus on problem-solving, we must also develop students' emotional intelligence. We must cultivate their ability to reflect on their strengths and weaknesses as well as their ability to understand and work with others (the intrapersonal and interpersonal intelligences, two of Howard Gardner's multiple intelligences). Working with and learning from others who are different poses different and often more difficult challenges, and these talents become even more important in an increasingly diverse world.

Perhaps the best vision for how all these skills come together is presented by Gardner in his book *Five Minds for the Future*. He makes the link among skills found in the left and right sides of the brain and weaves in the all-important components of responsibility and character. Gardner believes that success in the future will require that students have skills in five different areas: the disciplined mind, the synthesizing mind, the creative mind, the respectful mind, and the ethical mind. He states, "With these 'minds,' as I refer to them, a person will be well equipped to deal with what is expected, as well as what cannot be anticipated; without these minds, a person will be at the mercy of forces that he or she can't understand, let alone control."

Obstacles to the kinds of shifts I suggest typically fall into two camps, centering around intent and time. If intent is lacking — if school leaders do not see the need to change and address the areas I have described — nothing significant will happen. As the pace of change accelerates, however, and as needs become more and more obvious and transparent, it will be harder to ignore reality. Thus school leaders will most likely be aware of these needs. Indeed, because independent schools are subject to market forces, they are likely to be on the cutting edge of the kinds of changes that are necessary for recruiting and preparing students.

Having sufficient time will then become the problem, and you may find yourself saying, "I value all these areas but am already having trouble finding enough time to cover our present curriculum. How can I add these priorities?" That's a fair question because school leaders (myself included) do a great job of adding on activities and goals; we are not very good at abandoning them. This leads to one inescapable conclusion: Schools will need to lengthen the time their students attend class. How they do this will be up to them, and it will vary. Some schools will lengthen the school day by starting earlier or ending later. Perhaps their after-school programs will incorporate more of an academic focus. Other schools will extend their calendar, adding weeks of school at the beginning or the end of summer vacation (or both). Some schools may consider requiring attendance for a few hours on Saturday morning, as is done in some Asian countries and in the K.I.P.P. (Knowledge Is Power Program) charter schools. Indeed, some independent schools have already begun lengthening their week by adding Saturday classes. This movement may quickly gain momentum. Sooner than we can imagine, schools will move away from the agrarian-based calendar in order to increase students' opportunities to learn.

Students' parents, used to choosing among airlines and overnight delivery services, will expect to have the same kinds of choices when it comes to education. As parents become consumers of schools and bring a customer's mentality (which is not necessarily a bad thing), assessment will become a more important factor in curriculum and instruction. The increased capacity to measure and record will result in more things being measured and recorded. This may not necessarily be a positive change since some of the new factors being measured won't be all that significant. Nevertheless, if something can be measured, it will be measured and the measurements will be compared. Schools that pride themselves on developing enthusiasm for learning, an appreciation for diversity, or leadership skills will be asked to show the data that support their claims.

Over time, as competitive pressures become more common and obvious in and among all schools, the differences between public and private schools will become far less salient. Public schools will become more entrepreneurial and private-like. They will develop marketing plans, recruit students, charge tuition, and raise money (some public schools are already doing this). Likewise, private schools will become more like public schools, working to increase their racial and ethnic diversity, accepting a wider academic and socioeconomic range of students, providing more services to parents, and increasing their emphasis on measurable results. Charter schools straddle the line between public and private schools and will increasingly represent another form of competition. (The number of charter schools already exceeds the number of NAIS schools.) The number of e-schools will also increase exponentially, offering additional options to families and employment opportunities to teachers. Indeed, in *Disrupting Class: How Disruptive Innovation Will Change the Way the World Learns*, Christensen, Horn, and Johnson predict that "online courses [will] have a 25 percent market share in high schools" by approximately 2014.

Accompanying the increase in options and the competitiveness among all kinds of schools will come a broader definition of who can teach. The recognition for "board-certified teachers" is increasing in some areas, but far more teachers are coming to the classroom through less-traditional routes. For years, many independent schools have hired teachers who were not graduates of university teacher-training programs, and this possibility is increasingly becoming available to all schools. Offering an intense summer crash course for college graduates, Teach for America has the highest visibility. This model, with some variation, is being pursued by various cities, organizations, and schools. (The Shady Hill School in Cambridge, Massachusetts, has been operating a teacher-training program since the 1920s.) My opinion is that this is a positive development. It also means, however, that school leaders will invariably hire teachers with less formal training and experience. This has implications for how leaders will focus their efforts.

THE FUTURE OF LEADERSHIP

What do these changes mean for school leaders? First, roles will change, becoming even more multifaceted and, yes, even more challenging. The demands of the job will increase, and school leaders, even the best ones, will be far less able to go it alone. The leaders who are successful will succeed because they are able to develop and to draw from those around them. The notion of "distributed leadership" describes this well. Stemming from the idea of distributed intelligence described earlier in this chapter, distributed leadership simply means that strong leaders tap into others' strengths and share responsibilities. Good leaders accept — indeed, embrace — the fact that an important part of their role is helping develop the people around them.

Distributed leadership begins with the people who are identified on the organizational chart as playing some sort of administrative role. The list of candidates from whom a head of school can draw may seem endless: admissions director, assistant principal, assistant head of school, associate head of school, department chairs, grade-level representatives, director of development, business manager, director of operations, assistant head for institutional advancement, and so on. Distributed leadership begins with the head of school working closely with other administrators.

Beyond that, however, good leaders also tap into those who do not hold an administrative title. The mathematics teacher who truly understands child development and the third-grade teacher who knows the community, the art teacher who can give open and candid feedback and the development director who senses how the board works — all possess valuable skills and understanding. A good leader knows where to turn to address which issues. And, of course, skilled leaders also reach into the board of trustees and parent body for ideas and suggestions.

The head's confidantes and reasons for seeking counsel vary by personality, time, setting, and issue. What does not vary is that strong leaders open the door to problem-solving. They invite others to help them, and they are open even to those who come to the party without an invitation. Strong leaders take all the ideas, impressions, and feelings and forge a solution as best they can. It is probable that the solution will be better because others are involved; it is definite that the implementation will be better because others are involved. The prospects are always best when everyone becomes part of the solution.

Leadership is about relationships, and good leaders pride themselves on their ability to develop others and draw from their strengths.

SUMMARY

Much will be different in schools 20 and 30 years from now. Because of technology, activities we can barely imagine today will become commonplace. How long students attend school each year and to what age they remain enrolled may also change dramatically. What we teach students will change, as there will assuredly be dramatic shifts in both content and pedagogy. Where schools are housed — if they are housed at all — is subject to change as well. "Going to school" will have very different connotations if cars and buses are fueled by gasoline that costs $25 per gallon or by solar-powered machines, and either scenario is possible.

In what ways will the teaching force change? Will a premium on education lead to greater teacher pay, resulting in an increased ability to attract and keep the best and the brightest in the classroom? Or will curricular offerings reduce the skills teachers need? Will e-teaching enable the best teachers to present to scores or hundreds of students simultaneously? If so, to what degree?

Society will ask more of students, and schools will be forced to respond. While today's schools and classrooms have much in common with those attended by our present students' parents (and grandparents), this will not be the case in the future. Schools and classrooms in the year 2025 will be very different from those in 1990.

What won't change are the qualities that define leaders. Indeed, the increased reliance on technology and global communication will result in a greater need for leaders who listen and understand. In an even faster and more fragmented world, leaders who take the time to know their employees, leaders who take the time to explain, and leaders who take the time to involve others will be the leaders who make a difference.

APPENDIX

■

SPRING PARENT SURVEY

Dear Parents,

I want to hear from you! Please use this survey to share your thoughts about NCS: Give feedback, offer input, make suggestions. Some of these questions are open-ended, while others are forced-choice. Some of the latter are followed by an open-ended question to allow for your explanation.

Note that this survey is not anonymous (since your e-mail address is shown). If you wish to be anonymous, please print a hard copy and return it to me. Please indicate whether you would like a personal response from me.

1. Please indicate your child's grade in the current academic year.

☐ 3/4s

☐ 4/5s

☐ kindergarten

☐ 1st grade

☐ 2nd grade

☐ 3rd grade

☐ 4th grade

☐ 5th grade

☐ 6th grade

☐ I/we have more than one child at NCS

2. Why are you at NCS? Please check the MOST IMPORTANT reason(s) why your family is enrolled here.

☐ strong academics

☐ focus on the personal intelligences

☐ racial and socio-economic diversity

☐ family support (extended day)

☐ use of multiple intelligences (MI)

☐ location of NCS

☐ lower tuition than competitors

☐ other (if so, please share what this is in question #3)

3. Of the factors mentioned in Question 2, please write those that are essential to your decision to enroll your child at NCS.

_____

_____

_____

_____

4. Please indicate your agreement with the statement "My child's individual needs have been met." Question #5 allows you to elaborate.

☐ strongly agree

☐ agree

☐ DISagree

☐ strongly DISagree

5. Please explain your thinking in responding to question #4.

_____

_____

_____

_____

6. Please indicate your agreement with the statement "Tom has been friendly and supportive." (Yes, that's me!) Feel free to elaborate in question #18.

☐ strongly agree

☐ agree

☐ DISagree

☐ strongly DISagree

7. Please indicate your agreement with the statement "My parent-teacher conferences were productive." Feel free to elaborate in question #18.

☐ strongly agree

☐ agree

☐ DISagree

☐ strongly DISagree

8. How would you rank your interactions with our business office? Please add comments in question #9.

☐ good

☐ OK

☐ unsatisfactory

9. Please share your thinking in responding to question #8.

_____

_____

_____

_____

10. How would you rank your interactions with our development office? Please add comments in question #12.

_____

_____

_____

_____

11. Would you prefer to see the NCS annual report in a calendar form or as a regular annual report? Please share your thinking in #12.

☐ as a school calendar

☐ as an annual report

12. Please share your thinking in responding to question #10 and/or question #11.

_____

_____

_____

_____

13. Please react to the following statement: "The NCS Extended Day program is high quality." If you do not participate in our Extended Day program, what would you like to see happen so that you would use it?

_____

_____

_____

_____

14. What thoughts do you have about our specialists' programs? These include art, performing arts, Spanish, library, science, physical education, creative movement, learning specialist, computer, and counselor. (Not all students or grades have access to each of these programs.)

_____

_____

_____

_____

15. What do you see as NCS's major strengths?

_____

_____

_____

_____

16. What do you see as NCS's major weaknesses?

_____

_____

_____

_____

17. Please share any suggestions or ideas you have about how we might become a better school.

_____

_____

_____

_____

18. Do you have any other comments, observations, or questions? Please use this space to clarify any previous answers, and don't forget to let me know if you'd like a personal response from me.

_____

_____

_____

_____

Again, thanks.

BIBLIOGRAPHY

Anderson, Chris. *The Long Tail: Why the Future of Business Is Selling Less of More.* New York: Hyperion, 2006.

Barth, Roland S. *Improving Schools from Within.* San Francisco, Jossey-Bass, 1990.

Bassett, Patrick F. "Teacher Attributes and Needs." Originally published by ISACS, modified by NAIS, April 2002; online at *www.nais.org/about/article. cfm?ItemNumber=145397.*

Bornstein, Rita. *Legitimacy in the Academic Presidency: From Entrance to Exit.* Westport, CT: American Council on Education, Praeger, 2003.

Branch, Taylor. *Parting the Waters: America in the King Years, 1954-63.* New York: Simon & Schuster, 1988.

Brett, Jeanne, Kristin Behfar, and Mary C. Kern. "Managing Multicultural Teams." *Harvard Business Review,* November 2006.

Brooks, David. "The End of Integration." *New York Times,* July 6, 2007; online at *www. jacobsladder.name/interfaith/faith/faithfulmoderates/theendofintegration.htm.*

Carlson, Richard. "Succession and Performance Among School Superintendents." *Administrative Science Quarterly* 6, September 1961, pp. 210–227.

Chait, Richard P., William P. Ryan, and Barbara E. Taylor. *Governance as Leadership: Reframing the Work of Nonprofit Boards.* Hoboken, NJ: John Wiley, 2005.

Christensen, Clayton M., Michael B. Horn, and Curtis W. Johnson. *Disrupting Class: How Disruptive Innovation Will Change the Way the World Learns.* New York: McGraw-Hill, 2008.

Collins, Jim. *Good to Great and the Social Sectors: A Monograph to Accompany Good to Great.* New York: Collins Business, 2006.

Colson, Helen A. *Philanthropy at Independent Schools, Second Edition.* Washington, DC: National Association of Independent Schools, 2002.

Deal, Terrence E., and Kent D. Peterson. *Shaping School Culture: The Heart of Leadership.* San Francisco: Jossey-Bass, 1999.

Drucker, Peter F. *Managing the Nonprofit Organization: Principles and Practices*. New York: HarperCollins, 1990.

Dweck, Carol S. *Mindset: The New Psychology of Success*. New York: Random House, 2006.

Eisner, Elliot W. "Preparing for Today and Tomorrow." *Educational Leadership* 61, December 2003/January 2004, pp. 6–10.

Fishman, Ted C. *China, Inc.: How the Rise of the Next Superpower Challenges America and the World*. New York: Scribner, 2005.

Florida, Richard. *The Rise of the Creative Class … and How It's Transforming Work, Leisure, Community & Everyday Life*. New York: Basic Books, 2002.

Friedman, Thomas L. *The World Is Flat: A Brief History of the Twenty-First Century*. New York: Farrar, Straus and Giroux, 2005.

Gardner, Howard. *Five Minds for the Future*. Boston: Harvard Business School Publishing, 2006.

Gardner, Howard. *Frames of Mind: The Theory of Multiple Intelligences*. New York: Basic Books, 1983.

Goleman, Daniel. *Emotional Intelligence: Why It Can Matter More Than IQ*. New York: Bantam Books, 1995.

Goleman, Daniel. *Social Intelligence: The New Science of Human Relationships*. New York: Bantam Books, 2006.

Goodwin, Doris Kearns. *Team of Rivals: The Political Genius of Abraham Lincoln*. New York: Simon & Schuster, 2005.

Grace, Kay Sprinkel. *Beyond Fundraising: New Strategies for Nonprofit Innovation and Investment*, 2nd ed. Hoboken, NJ: Wiley, 2005.

Gurian, Michael, and Patricia Henley, with Terry Trueman. *Boys and Girls Learn Differently! A Guide for Teachers and Parents*. San Francisco: Jossey-Bass, 2001.

Herzberg, Frederick. *The Motivation to Work*. New York: Wiley, 1959.

Hill, Linda A. "Becoming the Boss." *Harvard Business Review*, January 2007, pp. 52–53.

Hoerr, Thomas R. *The Art of School Leadership.* Washington, DC: Association for Supervision and Curriculum Development, 2005.

Hoerr, Thomas R. "Consumers Versus Customers in School: What Are the Differences?" *Classroom Leadership,* September 2002.

Homans, George S. *Social Behavior: Its Elementary Forms.* New York: Harcourt Brace, 1961.

Hymowitz, Carol. "Reshaping: CEOs May Encounter Resistance in Changing Company Culture." *Wall Street Journal,* August 19, 2007; online at BNET Business Network.

Katz, Lucinda Lee, and Bonnie L. Wishne. *Awareness to Commitment to Action.* Independent Schools Association of the Central States (Spring 1997); online at *www.isacs.org/resources/monographs/library.asp?action=show&category=9&id=215.*

Kunstler, John Howard. *The Long Emergency: Surviving the Converging Catastrophes of the Twenty-First Century.* New York: Atlantic Monthly Press, 2005.

Kurzweil, Ray, and Terry Grossman. *Fantastic Voyage: Live Long Enough to Live Forever.* Emmaus, PA: Rodale, 2004.

Lancaster, Lynne C., and David Skillman. *When Generations Collide: Who They Are. Why They Clash. How to Solve the Generational Puzzle at Work.* New York: HarperCollins, 2002.

Levine, Mel. *A Mind at a Time.* New York: Simon & Schuster, 2002.

Levinson, Jay, and Seth Godin. *The Guerrilla Marketing Handbook.* Boston: Houghton Mifflin, 1994.

Lightfoot, Sara Lawrence. *The Good High School: Portraits of Character and Culture.* New York: Basic Books, 1983.

Maxwell, John C. *The 360 Degree Leader: Developing Your Influence from Anywhere in the Organization.* Nashville, TN: Thomas Nelson, 2005.

McHenry, Irene, Kay Edstene, Tom Farquhar, Harry Hammond, Laura Jackson, Juan Jewell, Michi Tashjian, and Norma Vogel. *Embracing the Tension: Evidence for Conflict as the Locus of Moral Growth. A Study of Moral Growth in Friends High Schools.* Philadelphia: Friends Council on Education, 1998.

Michelli, Joseph A. *The Starbucks Experience: 5 Principles for Turning Ordinary into Extraordinary.* New York: McGraw-Hill, 2007.

Murray, Charles. "Aztecs vs. Greeks." *Wall Street Journal*, January 18, 2007; online at *www.opinionjournal.com/extra/?id=110009541.*

Murray, Charles. "Intelligence in the Classroom." *Wall Street Journal*, January 16, 2007; online at *www.opinionjournal.com/extra/?id=110009531.*

Murray, Charles. "What's Wrong with Vocational School?" *Wall Street Journal*, January 17, 2007; online at *www.opinionjournal.com/extra/?id=110009535.*

New City School. *Celebrating Multiple Intelligences.* St. Louis, MO: New City School, 1992.

New City School. *Succeeding with Multiple Intelligences.* Missouri: St. Louis, MO: New City School, 1994.

O'Toole, James. *Leading Change: The Argument for Values-Based Leadership.* San Francisco: Jossey-Bass, 1995.

Peters, Thomas J., and Robert H. Waterman, Jr. *In Search of Excellence: Lessons from America's Best-Run Companies.* New York: HarperCollins, 1982.

Pink, Daniel H. *A Whole New Mind: Moving from the Information Age to the Conceptual Age.* New York: Riverhead Books, 2005.

Putnam, Robert D. *Bowling Alone: The Collapse and Revival of American Community.* New York: Simon & Schuster, 2000.

Raines, Claire. *Beyond Generation X: A Practical Guide for Managers.* Boston: Thomson Crisp Learning, 1997.

Reicher, Stephen D., Michael J. Platow, and S. Alexander Haslam. "The New Psychology of Leadership." *Scientific American Mind*, August/September 2007.

Ries, Al, and Laura Ries. *The 22 Immutable Laws of Branding: How to Build a Product or Service into a World-Class Brand.* New York: HarperCollins, 1998.

Senge, Peter M. *The Fifth Discipline: The Art and Practice of the Learning Organization.* New York: Currency Doubleday, 1990.

Smith, Adam. *Wealth of Nations.* London: Methuen & Co., 1904 (first published in 1776).

Smith, Alexander McCall. *The No. 1 Ladies' Detective Agency*. New York: Anchor Books, 1998.

Tatum, Beverly Daniel. *"Why Are All the Black Kids Sitting Together in the Cafeteria?" And Other Conversations About Race*. New York: Basic Books, 1997.

Thomson, Barbara J. *Words Can Hurt You: Beginning a Program of Anti-Bias Education*. Boston: Addison-Wesley, 1992.

Wagner, Tony. "Leadership for Learning: An Action Theory of School Change." *Phi Delta Kappan* 82, No. 5 (January 2001); online at *www.pdkintl.org/kappan/k0101wag. htm*.

ABOUT THE AUTHOR

Thomas R. Hoerr has led schools for more than 30 years and is a student of leadership and change. Since 1981, he has been the head of the New City School, an independent school in St. Louis, Missouri. NCS is a multiple intelligences school and attracts educational visitors from around the world. Previously, he served as a public school principal and teacher. Hoerr also directed and taught in the NonProfit Management Program at Washington University in St. Louis. He was a Klingenstein Fellow and holds a doctorate in educational policymaking and program development from Washington University in St. Louis.

Hoerr is the author of two other books, *Becoming a Multiple Intelligences School* (ASCD Press, 2000) and *The Art of School Leadership* (ASCD Press, 2005). He writes a bimonthly column for *Educational Leadership*, "The Principal Connection." More than 70 of his articles have been published in magazines and journals, including *Education Week*, *Teachers College Record*, *Kappan*, *Educational Leadership*, *Principal*, *Independent School*, *EQ Australia*, *Early Childhood Today*, and *Parent and Child*.

Hoerr presents at conferences and schools and has spoken in the United States as well as in Australia, New Zealand, Great Britain, Canada, Argentina, Chile, Hong Kong, Singapore, and Denmark. Readers who have questions or wish to continue the dialogue can contact Tom at *trhoerr@newcityschool.org*.